TRANSFORMING ECONOMIC LIFE
A Millennial Challenge

James Robertson studied classics, history and philosophy at Oxford. He worked in Whitehall and accompanied Harold Macmillan on his prime-ministerial "Wind of Change" tour of Africa in 1960. After directing the Inter-Bank Research Organisation and contributing to enquiries on government, civil service, parliament and London's future as a financial centre, he became an independent writer and lecturer. Since 1975 he and his wife Alison Pritchard (a Schumacher Society Council member), have issued the twice-yearly *Turning Point* (latterly *Turning Point 2000*) newsletter. They helped to set up The Other Economic Summit (TOES) and the New Economics Foundation in 1984/5.

His 1998 Liverpool Schumacher Lecture was on 'After Dependency: Healthy People And Places In The 21st Century'. His latest book, *Beyond the Dependency Culture*, has just been published (Adamantine Press, 1998). This present Briefing covers some of the issues raised in his 1997 Briefing for Policy Makers on *A New Economics of Sustainable Development*, written for the European Commission.

Schumacher Briefing No. 1

TRANSFORMING ECONOMIC LIFE
A Millennial Challenge

James Robertson

published by Green Books
for The Schumacher Society
in association with The New Economics Foundation

First published in 1998
by Green Books Ltd
Foxhole, Dartington, Totnes,
Devon TQ9 6EB

for The Schumacher Society
Foxhole, Dartington, Totnes,
Devon TQ9 6EB

in association with The New Economics Foundation
1st Floor, Vine Court, 112-116 Whitechapel Road,
London E1 1JE. UK Registered Charity no. 1055254

Cover design by Rick Lawrence

Printed by J.W. Arrowsmith Ltd
Bristol, UK

A catalogue record for this publication is available
from the British Library

ISBN 1 870098 72 2

CONTENTS

Foreword

I am proud to present James Robertson's *Transforming Economic Life: A Millennial Challenge*, the first Schumacher Briefing. It is James's outstanding achievement to put forward a thesis on a sustainable economy for the 21st century that is both visionary and practical. It acknowledges that people need to have the chance to anchor themselves in their own local economies as a basis for a sustainable livelihood, whilst humanity also needs to be in touch worldwide. It also implies that instead of adjusting nature to fit in with our behaviour patterns, we have to adjust our economic practices to be compatible with the natural world.

Since the 1970s, James Robertson has been a pioneer in developing a new economics of sustainability. It is his unique capacity to both envision and to synthesise leading edge ideas that make this a document of a very special quality. I wish to thank James for writing this first Schumacher Briefing.

It is being published by Green Books for the Schumacher Society. E.F. Schumacher, who died in 1977, was one of the first people to talk about sustainable development. His special contribution was to explain that the gigantism of modern economic systems tends to diminish the well-being of individuals and communities, and the health and diversity of the natural world.

In the last two decades it has become increasingly apparent that Schumacher helped lay the foundations for a profound reworking of the values and priorities of western industrial society which is continuing today. His work was theoretical as well as practical: he was a founder of Intermediate Technology and was president of the Soil Association. His ideas were first aired by Resurgence magazine and they are at the heart of the New Economics Foundation. Schumacher College at Dartington, was founded in his name. Together with the Schumacher Society, all these organisations have joined in the Schumacher Circle: together we want to change the core values of contemporary society so that social, economic and ecological issues are approached, and solutions devised, 'as if people matter'.

We recognise that human thought has created the profoundly unstable world in which we now live, which is manifested in mega-technology, global power structures and vast environmental impacts. The importance of Schumacher's contribution to sustainable development is reflected in the fact that Societies in his name have also been founded in Germany and the USA. We are in close touch with our sister organisations and are planning to run shared events in the future.

The Schumacher Society will publish at least three Briefings a year. The next one, written by myself, on sustainable settlements, will be published in October 1998. We aim to produce ground-breaking documents of incisive quality that address key issues of our time. It is our purpose to inspire readers with practical visions and working examples of innovative, alternative systems and to help spread new thinking on sustainability, peace and personal empowerment.

I wish to thank John Elford, a Council member of the Schumacher Society, and Managing Director of Green Books, for taking on the task of publishing the Schumacher Briefings. As usual, John has made a tremendous effort to bring out a document we can all feel proud of.

The Briefings will be on sale to the public, but will also be available direct to members of the Schumacher Society as part of our regular mailings (details of membership are given on page 78). If you feel that this Briefing is helpful to you in your own work, please recommend it to friends and colleagues.

Thank you for taking the time to read *Transforming Economic Life*. We are very pleased to publish this Briefing in association with the New Economics Foundation, of which James Robertson was a founder. NEF has pioneered the new thinking on economics which is now making significant inroads into academia and into economic policy. This is indeed a *Millennial Challenge*, and we are pleased to contribute to the process.

Herbert Girardet
Chairman, Schumacher Society

Acknowledgements

I want to express my very warm thanks to Herbert Girardet who invited me to write this Briefing and to John Elford who saw it through printing in record time; and also to Ed Mayo of the New Economics Foundation. They all read the text in draft and suggested important improvements of substance and presentation. They are not, of course, to blame for the failings that remain.

INTRODUCTION & SUMMARY

"We need freedom and order: the freedom of lots and lots of small units and the order of large-scale, possibly global, organisation." E.F. Schumacher[1]

It is a pleasure to have been invited to write this first Schumacher Briefing. I knew Fritz Schumacher personally, and had the privilege of speaking on the same platform with him several times. I vividly remember a copy of his last book, *A Guide for the Perplexed*, arriving in the mail with the author's compliments the morning after I heard of his death. Shortly afterwards I took his place on some speaking engagements in Canada. In general our thinking was very compatible. Re-reading him now, twenty years after his death, confirms how relevant and fresh his ideas still are.

Aims
A great variety of activities now reflect people's growing commitment to people-centred, ecologically sustainable development—new lifestyles, new technologies, new enterprises, new approaches to business management, and so on. On the negative side, the conventional ways of evaluating economic decisions and progress are deeply misconceived, and the present economic system has inherent tendencies to destroy the natural environment, to destroy community, to transfer wealth from poor to rich, to marginalise people, communities and cultures, to erode and deny the sense of the spiritual or sacred, and to create learned incapacity and helplessness.[2] This Briefing takes those realities as its starting point. It looks forward to a future when we will be better able to control our economic destinies, and to treasure the blessings of nature on which we all depend. It focuses on some specific changes which will help to bring that future about.

---

1. In 'The New Economics', *Resurgence*, Sept/Oct 1968, republished in Schumacher, E.F. (1997).
2. These failings were outlined by the late Willis Harman and Thomas J. Hurley of the Institute of Noetic Sciences in a 1996 Progress Report from their study entitled *Pathfinding Collaborative Inquiry*.

In such a future, many households and local communities will produce a greater proportion of the things they need, like food and energy, than today. They will be more reliant on themselves and one another, and less dependent on big businesses and financial institutions and government services. In particular, they will be less dependent on employers to organise their work and provide their incomes. More people will do more of their work at home and close to home. For other purposes also, communication may increasingly provide an alternative to travel. There will be less long-distance transportation of freight, as local production for local consumption becomes more nearly the norm. Education will prepare people not just for jobs, but to manage their lives—including their households, family life, work, money, and roles and responsibilities as citizens. Active citizenship—local, national and global—will play a larger part in many people's lives than today. Many will experience life as saner and less stressful, as they become more deeply involved in their local communities and more closely connected with the natural world. In ways that will differ from today's, more people will be better able to satisfy their needs—for subsistence, protection, participation, esteem, meaning, identity, freedom and self-actualisation—without preventing other people from satisfying theirs.[3]

Against that background, the Briefing focuses on certain changes that are crucial to the transition to a people-centred, ecologically sustainable economy. These are framework or system changes. They are primarily to do with money. Three major initiatives are suggested.

Analysis

Chapter 1 aims to convey the systemic nature of the transformation needed to turn the present economic system into a 21st-century economy "as if people and the Earth matter", and the principles which will underlie it. It indicates how the roles of the state, the market and the citizen will differ in a people-centred economy from their roles in today's business-centred and government-centred economies. It describes how the web of interactions between different parts of the economic system creates an ecology of change (and

---

3. On needs, see Maslow (1970) and Max-Neef in Ekins (1986).

inertia), and the need to transcend the fragmented capacities of government departments and academic institutes.

Three examples of the need for a systemic approach are discussed:

- seeing the economic system as a circular, not a linear process;
- breaking into the self-reinforcing, positive feedback trap of consumption-must-grow, production-must-grow and money-must-grow; and
- treating the world economy, no longer as a collection of competing national economies, but as a one-world, decentralising economic system.

Chapter 2 shows that restructuring taxation and public spending will encourage a desirable new direction of progress in many sectors of the economy. Sectors discussed include food and farming; travel and transport; energy; work, livelihoods and social inclusion; technology; business; health, and law and order.

Reform of Public Finance

Chapter 3 therefore explores the scope for a fundamental reform of public finance. It suggests:

- a combined programme over a period of years—to raise energy, land and environmental taxes; reduce taxes on employment, incomes, profits, value-added and saving; and introduce a Citizen's Income. (This will embody a new social compact: people will pay for what they take out of the common pot, not for what they contribute to it; and all citizens will have a right to share in the proceeds.)
- the termination, again over a period of years, of the £billions of perverse subsidies that now skew prices in favour of socially and environmentally damaging activities. (Temporary subsidies for such things as organic farm conversions and environmental investment are suggested.)

These and other proposed changes in public finance reflect a vision of a people-centred society, whose citizens are more equal with one another in terms of esteem, capability and material conditions of life than now, and less dependent on big business and government to meet their needs.

Wider Monetary and Financial Reforms

Chapter 4 is about the money system itself. It is increasingly experienced as incomprehensible, unaccountable, irresponsible, exploitative and out of control. Its effects are socially and ecologically destructive, and economically inefficient. It systematically transfers wealth from poor to rich people, places and countries. The money-must-grow imperative pushes production and consumption to higher and higher levels; and it skews economic effort towards making money out of money, rather than providing necessary goods and services.

Some specific innovations, such as local currencies and LETS (Local Exchange Tradings Systems), microcredit, community credit unions, local investment banks, ethical (social and green) investment, and the application of social and environmental accounting and auditing procedures to financial institutions, must be vigorously supported and spread.

However, by themselves they will not transform the mainstream money system, and that is where change is needed. The problems are that money is conceptually slippery, it is shrouded in professional mystery, managing it confers power, and electronic money raises new questions for the future. It has been difficult for policy makers in other fields, and for NGOs, to get to grips with the changes needed. But working out a strategy for change, and mobilising support for it, is a top priority. This is one of the most creative and crucial tasks facing the new economics movement.

The Emerging Global Economy

The thrust of economic globalisation today, dominated by an alliance of multinational corporations, rich-country governments and world-level institutions like the IMF, is intolerable. But we live in one world. Most of us want to take part in its rich social, cultural and geographical diversity. Most of us recognise that global economic problems must be tackled, and that we cannot withdraw altogether into small self-sufficient local community economies of our own. Chapter 5, then, is about creating a one-world economic system which will positively encourage self-reliant peoples, communities and nations to conserve Earth's resources for the benefit of all.

For the peoples of Britain and other rich countries this will mean three things. We must reorientate our own way of economic life. We must help other peoples to do the same by the way we manage our international trade, investment and aid. And, with other members of the international community, we must evolve new global policies to regulate trade, develop a system of global taxation, manage the international monetary and financial system including international debts, and restructure and democratise the institutions of global economic governance.

Summary

The Briefing makes three proposals.

The first is for a campaign to transform public finance, as outlined in Chapter 3. This could be led by a coalition of NGOs concerned with food, farming, travel, transport and other sectors discussed in Chapter 2.

The second is to define a strategy, covering the issues discussed in Chapter 4, to transform the existing system of money and finance.

The third is to step up support for the efforts already being made by international NGOs to transform the existing policies and institutions of global economic governance, as outlined in Chapter 5.

There are links between these proposals. But for practical purposes it will be best to tackle them separately until they are well under way. I hope that other NGOs, as well as the Schumacher Society and the New Economics Foundation, will take them up, together with active private individuals, and people in government, academic institutions and the professions.

For many millions of people the late 20th-century world economic system is violent and destructive, unfree and disorderly. We must transform it into a 21st-century system designed and able to meet the needs of people and the Earth, including their needs for freedom and peace and order. This Briefing is a contribution to that task. I believe that, had Fritz Schumacher still been living, he would have endorsed the suggestions it makes.

Chapter 1
TRANSFORMING THE SYSTEM

"An economic system is not only an institutional device for satisfying existing wants and needs but a way of fashioning wants in the future."
John Rawls [1]

Principles

Today's economic system must be transformed into a 21st-century economy "as if people and the Earth matter".[2] Many people see this transformation as one aspect of a larger historical change—the end of the modern age and the transition to a post-modern age, marked by a new awareness of our common humanity and our kinship with the rest of creation.

The principles underlying it will contrast with the principles of conventional economics today. They will include the following:

• systematic empowerment of people, as opposed to making and keeping them dependent;
• systematic conservation of resources and environment;
• evolution from a 'wealth of nations' model of economic life to a one-world model, and from today's international economy to a decentralising multi-level one-world economic system;
• restoration of political and ethical choice to a central place in economic life and thought, based on respect for qualitative values, not just quantitative ones; and
• respect for feminine values, not just masculine ones.

Our approach must be based on action—to create a better future for people and the Earth. Economics cannot avoid being normative. Nature abhors a vacuum, and the vacuum created by the pretensions of conventional economics to be an objective, value-free science has been filled by values of power and greed.

In contrast to 20th-century economic orthodoxy, the 21st-century economy must be based on a realistic view of human nature. People

---

1. Rawls, J. (1971), *A Theory of Justice*, Oxford University Press.
2. "Economics as if people mattered" was the subtitle of E.F. Schumacher's best-known book *Small Is Beautiful*.

are altruistic as well as selfish, co-operative as well as competitive. R.H. Tawney's argument, that economic institutions should reward socially benign activities and so make the better choice the easier choice, makes sense. (But we should not dream, in Gandhi's words, of systems so perfect that no-one will need to be good.)

Our perspective should be dynamic and developmental, not static. Our task is to change the direction of progress, not to achieve a permanent destination or lay out a blueprint for a once-for-all 21st-century Utopia.

The State, the Market and the Citizen

There is not, never has been, nor ever could be, a completely free market economy. If an economy started by being wholly unregulated, some people would soon become powerful enough to destroy the freedom of others, and the free market would quickly become unfree. On the other hand, economies subject to detailed intervention by government soon become inefficient and corrupt. What is needed is a market economy operating freely within a well-designed framework of government, law and money (including taxes and public spending). By that framework, and how it influences prices throughout the economy, the state should aim to bring economic activity into harmony with society's values.

So, what should the framework be designed to achieve? The answer is: it should empower and encourage people, communities, and nations to take more control over their own economic destinies, to become more economically self-reliant, and to live in ways that are environmentally benign. The changes this requires include changes of relationship between state, market and citizen.

Twentieth-century political debate and conflict has focused around three types of economy:

• a state-centred command economy;
• a business-centred free-market economy; and
• a mixed economy, in which economic power and influence are shared between government, business and trade unions—the 'social partners', in the idiom of continental Europe.

As suggested in Diagrams 1 and 2, all these have been based on a producer-centred, employer-centred model of the economic system,

Diagram 1
THE BIG BROTHER ECONOMY

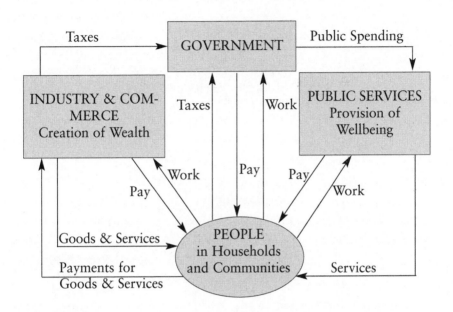

which differs crucially from the people-centred (or citizen-centred) model needed for the 21st century.

The collapse of communism is not "the end of history" and the start of permanent rule by conventional free-market capitalism. The reverse is true. Removal of the threat of Soviet state-dominated communism means that the non-communist world need no longer, in Hilaire Belloc's words, "keep a-hold of Nurse for fear of finding something worse". Future historians will see the collapse of communism as the first of two major changes that brought the producer-orientated economic development of the late modern era to an end. It opens the way to the transformation of Western business-dominated capitalism too.

Market and state will both continue to play vital parts in a people-centred economy. But activities carried out neither for profit in the market nor by employees of the state will also help to shape economic and social progress in the 21st century. A growing informal

Diagram 2
**A PEOPLE-CENTRED
ECONOMY**

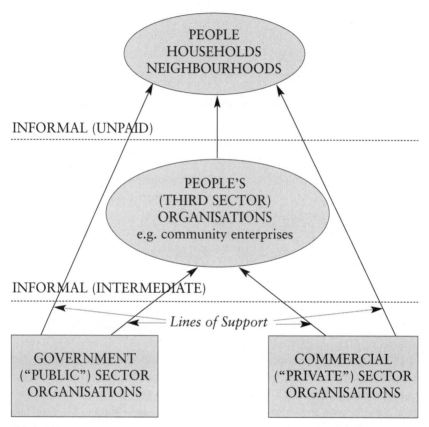

economy, based on unpaid, interpersonal co-operative self-reliance, will be supported by a growing third sector of non-profit, non-state organisations distinct from the conventional "public" and "private" sectors. The province of citizen activity, free from the impersonal constraints of the state and the market under conventional communism/socialism and capitalism, will grow. The 20th-century economy has given priority to the interests of business and finance, employers and trade unions, government and other organisations, assuming that people must depend on them as consumers and employees in a production-centred dependency culture ("I shop, therefore I am", "I have a job, therefore I am"). 21st-century economic and social debate will go beyond the dependency culture. It will focus on the needs and rights and responsibilities of people as persons and citizens. Hence the significance of the proposed Citizen's Income.

The Need For A Systemic Approach
A comprehensive transformation of economic life and thought will involve:

• every sector, such as farming and food, travel and transport, and others discussed in Chapter 2;
• every level: personal and household, neighbourhood and local community, district and city, regional (sub-national), national, continental and global; and
• every feature—such as lifestyle choices and values, technological innovation, governmental and other organisational goals and policies, methods of measurement and valuation such as accounting, and the theoretical basis for economic teaching and research.

The web of interconnections, relationships and interactions between all of these can be understood as an 'ecology of change' and, conversely, an 'ecology of inertia'. Change achieved in one area (e.g energy use, or how economic success is measured) will help to ease change in others (e.g. agriculture, or transport), and change frustrated in one will help to frustrate it in others. So a synergistic approach is called for. The conventional departmental structure of governments and government agencies, and the departmentalisation of faculties and disciplines in universities and research institutes, are obstacles to this. The creative changes, on which the shift to a people-centred, environmentally sustainable economy will depend, must continue to come largely from NGOs, citizens' groups and other outsiders, and not from governmental, professional and academic establishments.

The need, then, is not just to tackle a multitude of separate economic problems, but to change the way the economic system works as a whole. The three following examples illustrate this.

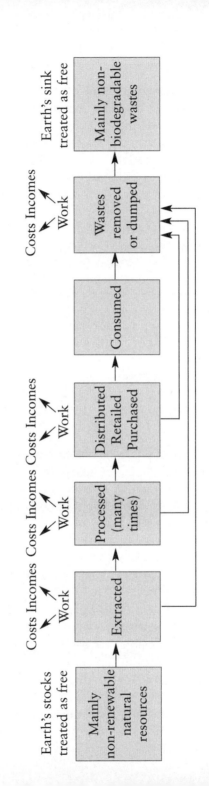

Diagram 3
THE ECONOMIC SYSTEM: LINEAR MODE

Diagram 4

THE ECONOMIC SYSTEM: CIRCULAR MODE

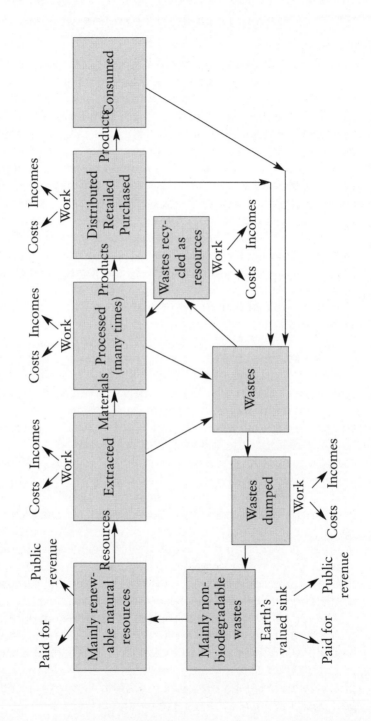

The Ecological Economy As A Circular System

Conventional economics has been based on a linear model of economic activities (as in Diagram 3). Material resources are extracted from Nature's supposedly unlimited pool, outside the economic system; they are then processed stage by stage into the eventual manufacture of consumer goods; those are then distributed and consumed, and the final wastes are dumped in Nature's unlimited sink, again outside the economic system. The capacity of Nature's resource pool and the capacity of Nature's waste sink have been treated as free goods, of no value. Values and costs, it has been assumed (the labour theory of value), arise only from the human work and enterprise involved in extracting the resources, processing them into goods, distributing them to consumers, and disposing of the wastes. Paradoxically, in the course of time it has been the fruits of human work and enterprise that have come to bear the main burden of taxation.

Land is one of the most important natural resources. From time to time past thinkers like Thomas Paine at the end of the 18th century and Henry George at the end of the 19th have argued that land does have a value and that landowners should pay rent to the community for it. But this has so far been successfully resisted by the rich and powerful, whose wealth and power has been based on their having 'enclosed' the value of land and other natural resources in their own countries—and as colonial and post-colonial powers in the world economy. Their resistance has had the backing of political theorists like John Locke, and by most professional economists—the great majority of whom have been directly or indirectly in their employment. But now, as taxation of energy, resources and pollution climbs higher up the agenda of sustainable development, and as pressure grows for greater economic democracy and social inclusion alongside conventional political democracy, the case for taxing land along with other resources will become stronger.

The economic system will look very different when understood as a circular system, as Diagram 4 suggests. It will then be seen, no longer as a machine attached externally to the natural world, but as an integral part of it, consisting of countless interrelated circular subprocesses so designed that wastes provide resources for other subprocesses and are reduced to a minimum. Value will be attributed to natural resources, including the environment's capacity to absorb waste and pollution. People and organisations using them or monopolising them will pay for the value they subtract by doing so, instead of being taxed on the values they add by their work and enterprise. The resulting higher costs of resource use and pollution (and lower costs of employing human effort and skills) will stimulate greater technical efficiency in the use of resources, and greater attention to reducing demand for them. Today's levels of resource use, wastage and pollution need to be reduced by 90%—"factor 10"—in countries like Britain before the end of the 21st century (Sachs 1998, p40).

Consumption, Production, Finance—An Interlocking System

Much attention, from the UN Development Programme downwards, is currently being given to 'sustainable consumption'. But preaching to consumers to mend their ways verges on 'blaming the victim'. Some of us have some power to consume less than we now do. But the present economic system makes this difficult for most people. Sustainable consumption cannot be treated as a self-contained goal.

As Diagram 5 suggests, so long as consumers remain trapped, along with producers and financial institutions, in today's system of imperatives (consumption-must-grow, because production-must-grow, because money-must-grow and jobs-must-be-provided), the continuing catastrophic growth of consumption is inevitable. Non-stop commercial advertising to maximise consumer spending on goods and services, reinforced by propaganda from government, business, the media, professional economists and economic commentators continually ramming it home that economic growth and rising high street sales are a 'good thing', reflects the production-must-grow imperative. That, in its turn, reflects the money-must-grow pressures on business managers from their shareholders, employees, and competitors and potential predators in the increasingly ruthless global financial jungle. In its turn, the money-must-grow imperative, articulated by the financial services industry, financial commentators and journalists, together with the government's emphasis on national Income (GDP) growth, is reinforced by the central role of interest and debt in the existing money and finance system (and scoring high money-numbers is a game that grabs the masculine mind).

Diagram 5
THE GROWTH TRAP

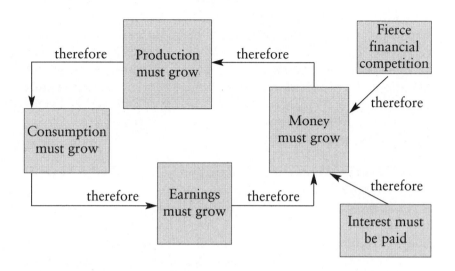

Towards A One-World Economic System

We now need to see the world economy as a single world economic system. As suggested in Diagram 6, it must be purposefully designed as a multi-level system which is decentralising as well as globalising—more self-reliant but more co-operative, more diverse but more unified, freer but more orderly, than today's free-for-all (free-for-some!) globalising economy. This new model reflects the emerging demand for new economic and monetary institutions (such as taxes and currencies) both at local and at supranational (e.g. European and global) levels. Those should no longer be seen as exceptional bells and whistles on the familiar 'wealth of nations' model of the economic world (like the Ptolemaic epicycles piled on epicycles of medieval astronomy). The 21st-century world economy must reflect the emerging consciousness of people as citizens of the world and of the locality where they live, as well as of their nation.

Its institutional structure must be designed to facilitate self-reliance for people and localities and nations. It should provide them with a degree of built-in protection and insulation from external economic instabilities outside their control. If it were a question of

Diagram 6
THE REDISTRIBUTION OF POLITICAL
& ECONOMIC POWER

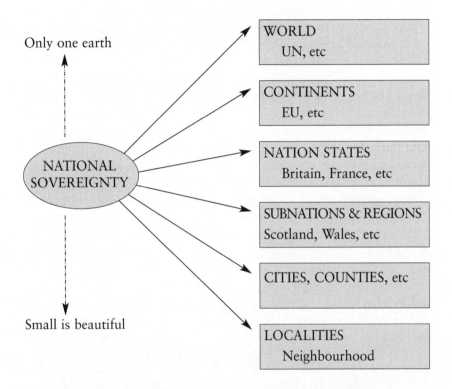

mechanical or electrical design, we would talk of buffering or insulating mechanisms, recognising that "coupled sub-systems are most stable when the coupling is rather weak. When the degree of coupling exceeds a certain level, the whole system can become violently unstable" (Roberts, 1985). In biological systems, devices like membranes filter and buffer the exchanges between subsystems, enabling them to function quasi-autonomously—being parts of larger wholes and at the same time having component subsystems of their own. We need not pursue these mechanical and biological analogies and metaphors too far. The point is that stable, well-functioning systems, including economic systems, allow their sub-systems enough autonomy and insulation from turbulence elsewhere in the system to enable them to continue functioning satisfactorily in troubled times.

From Commanding Heights To System Change

The 20th-century capitalist/socialist struggle has revolved around who shall control the 'commanding heights' of the economy—big finance and big business, or big government. The challenge of the 21st-century is to evolve an economic system which cannot be 'commanded' by any interest group, but is designed to secure economic freedom, self-reliance and democracy for all.

Linked with changes in culture and values, and laws and regulations, three key types of change affecting economic behaviour will help to transform today's economic system. The first is changes in financial instruments such as taxes and public subsidies which, by changing the streams of money between government and the rest of society, will help to change relative prices throughout the economy. The second is changes in how money itself works, and how this affects economic behaviour and outcomes. The third is changes in institutions—at local, national and supranational levels.

These changes are explored further in later chapters. They should be designed to reverse the effects of 'enclosure'. The exclusion of most people in the world from their share of the value of common resources developed by nature and society at large, and the enjoyment of that value by a privileged minority (including the writer and most readers of this Briefing) who have played no part in creating them, is the underlying cause of much of today's poverty and inequality, and an important cause of much environmental destruction.

They should also provide people, localities and nations with built-in levels of protection and insulation from instabilities in the national and global economy outside their control, enabling them to maintain their livelihoods when times are bad elsewhere.

Finally, they should apply universally and be transparent and simple. In other words, they should apply to everyone, and not be targeted at particular groups or interests. They should not result in a proliferation of overlapping regulations, taxes, benefits and subsidies. Ad hoc government interventions should be reduced to a minimum. How the economy's institutional framework operates, and how it affects prices and costs throughout the economy, should be clear to all.

A simpler and better designed regulatory and financial framework on those lines will allow the market economy to operate more fairly and freely and flexibly than today. As, in John Rawls' words, "an institutional device for fashioning wants", the economic system will then provide a more humane basis for human life, and encourage greater respect for the rest of the living world.

Chapter 2

A COMMON PATTERN

"We do not use a different scheme, a different framework, on each occasion. It is the essence of the matter that we use the same framework on different occasions."   P.F. Strawson[1]

Hitherto, most of the policy-makers, policy analysts, economists and other social science professionals, activists in NGOs and citizens' movements, and individual citizens, who want to help to create a more humane and ecological future, have naturally tended to focus primarily on their own particular field. Examples include food and farming; travel and transport; energy; work, livelihoods, and social inclusion; regeneration and development of local communities; new technological developments; transformation of business; a healthier society; and law and order. This chapter shows that a common set of framework changes, summarised in Box 1 overleaf, will encourage desirable change in them all.

Farming And Food
The existing food system fails to eliminate hunger, create food security, and enable people, localities and nations to achieve food self-reliance. Present methods of food production and distribution damage the environment and people's health. Changes are needed at international, national, local and household levels.

These should include more local growing of food for local consumption, as an aspect of more self-reliant rural and urban economies. That will reduce 'food miles'—the distance food travels between producers and consumers—and that in turn will reduce the use of energy and the pollution associated with long-distance transport. More people should be encouraged to grow more food for themselves and their families in gardens and allotments. These changes should be accompanied by a shift to more organic, less chemical and other less energy-intensive methods of food production; healthier food growing and food distribution; and more opportunities for employment in agriculture and horticulture. Finally, we

---

1. P.F. Strawson, *Individuals: An Essay in Descriptive Metaphysics*, Methuen 1959.

Box 1: Some Examples of Framework Changes
• Restructuring the tax system to encourage employment, environmentally benign development, and greater fairness.
• Introducing a Citizen's Income paid unconditionally to all citizens in place of tax reliefs and many existing welfare benefits.
• Terminating subsidies and other public expenditure programmes which encourage dependency-creating and environmentally unsustainable development.
• Introducing public purchasing policies which encourage contractors to adopt equitable and sustainable practices.
• Developing more self-reliant local economies.
• Developing new indicators to measure economic, social and environmental performance and progress.
• Developing accounting, auditing and reporting procedures to monitor organisations' social and environmental performance.
• Reducing demand, not just improving supply, for such things as transport, energy, jobs, health services, police and prisons.

need a fairer international trading regime, enabling all countries to achieve greater food security in more secure and sustainable national economies.

The proposals in Box 1 will lead to price changes throughout the food system that will support those developments. For example, shifting taxes away from employment and incomes on to energy use and pollution will directly encourage most of them. So will the removal of existing subsidies which damage the environment, raise land values artificially, encourage reductions in agricultural employment and favour capital- and energy-intensive farming, favour rich farmers against poorer ones (so encouraging the amalgamation of small farms into big ones and making it difficult for new people to start up in farming unless they are rich), and undermine food production and food security in developing countries by encouraging the dumping of excess food on to the world market.[2] A Citizen's

---

2. Specific implications for the European Common Agricultural Policy (CAP) were summarised in a 4-page Briefing Note of November 1996 jointly produced by SAFE (Sustainable Agriculture, Food and Environment Alliance) and CIIR (Catholic Institute for International Relations). A proposed rewording of Article 39 of the Treaty of European Union to formulate new objectives for the CAP was published by WWF Europe in January 1996.

Box 2: The Meaning of Efficiency

Efficiency is measured as a ratio between significant inputs and significant outputs; the greater the output in relation to the input, the greater the efficiency. So its meaning depends on what are seen as the most significant inputs and outputs—what inputs are most important to reduce, and what outputs are most important to increase? In farming and every other sphere it has been assumed efficient to reduce labour. Supposedly efficient farms have produced high profits (output) compared with the number of workers employed (input). Ratios between the calorific value of the food produced and the materials used to produce it, or between the amount of food produced and the area of land farmed, have not been seen as significant. Nor have the externalised costs of water, air and land pollution, soil erosion, impacts on human health, destruction of wildlife and wildlife habitats, and rural unemployment. The meaning of economic efficiency needs rethinking in all sectors of economic activity.

Income will help small farmers on low-value land, people starting employment (including part-time employment) in agriculture and horticulture, and people growing food unpaid in their gardens, allotments, etc. There may also be a case for temporary subsidies for organic farm conversions.

The new price and cost structures arising from the proposals in Box 1 will significantly reduce the financial incentives which now encourage factory farming to treat animals unnaturally and inhumanely—in their breeding, feeding (witness BSE), transport and slaughter. They could also provide some encouragement for vegetarianism, as well as for organic mixed farming.

Among issues of more general significance raised by the future of farming are efficiency and biotechnology. These are outlined in Boxes 2 and 3.

Travel And Transport

Conventional development in travel and transport damages the environment, and benefits richer people at the expense of poorer. New roads and airport runways benefit the people who use them and profit the companies which build them, but damage the

Box 3: Biotechnology and Genetically Engineered Life-Forms.
Dependency creation has been a feature of all conventional technological innovation—see page 37. The commercial development, patenting and monopolisation of existing and new animal and vegetable life-forms may be seriously damaging, not just environmentally but also economically and socially. The environmental impacts of releasing new life-forms cannot be predicted or controlled. The economic and social impacts will almost inevitably be dependency-creating and divisive. In India, for example, the Green Revolution involved "a shift from a farming system controlled by peasants to one controlled by agrichemical and seed corporations" (Shiva 1991, p64). Poorer peasants could not afford the new seeds and the machinery, fertilisers and pesticides to grow them, and had to become paid labourers of richer farmers. The commercial monopolisation of Earth's biodiverse genetic inheritance is an unacceptable "enclosure of the commons". The proposed framework changes in Box 1 will tend to reduce the financial attractions of commercial development of this type. But tough regulation will be needed too.

environment and the quality of life of people who cannot afford to use a car or travel by air. A society physically, socially and economically structured around motor transport means loss of opportunity, liberty and quality of life for people without cars—especially children, women and elderly people—for whom cars make the streets unpleasant and dangerous. 'Tourism concern' is about the damage caused to the environment and quality of life (especially of poorer people) in tourist destinations (especially in developing countries), while the benefits go mostly to visitors, and often to businesses, based elsewhere.

Changes must include a reduction in the need for mobility and thus in the demand for travel and transport. This will mean less mobile patterns of working, living and trading (with less long-distance commuting and freight transport), and planning and designing the built environment to make shops, schools, hospitals, offices and factories more accessible. Shifting from road and air to rail, water, cycling and walking, and from individual car travel to collective (e.g. bus and train) travel, must be encouraged. Greater technical efficiency in transport systems, reducing energy use and pollution, and improving safety standards and convenience, must be made profitable.

Again the proposals in Box 1 will lead to price changes favouring those developments. Shifting taxation away from employment and incomes on to energy use and pollution, and removing perverse subsidies, will encourage less travel and transport and more environmentally benign forms of them. Higher costs of long-distance transport and travel for business and trade will encourage more self-reliant local economies. By encouraging work in and around people's homes and neighbourhoods, the Citizen's Income will help to reduce travel to and from work.

Energy

Energy, like land, is a basic resource. It is required for all economic activity. But cheap fossil-fuel and nuclear energy is a cause of socially and environmentally damaging development. It replaces human usefulness with energy-intensive processes—processes that cause most types of pollution. It is calculated that, if the value derived from using energy were fairly shared between people living in all parts of the world, now and in the future, the industrialised countries would have to cut their use of fossil-fuel energy by up to 90%.

As with transport and travel, the need is both to reduce overall demand for energy and to replace environmentally and socially damaging types of energy supply with benign ones. This will mean shifting to new, less energy-intensive and transport-intensive patterns of production and consumption, living and working. It will mean greater technical efficiency so that less energy, and less polluting forms of energy, can provide high-standard products and services—heating, refrigeration, cooking, lighting, power, etc. (see von Weiszacker et al ,1997). And it will mean

- shifting from non-renewable fossil-fuel energy to renewable solar sources;
- replacing large centralised power stations and electricity grids—which are inefficient in terms of energy inputs and outputs, and over which people and local communities can exercise little control—with decentralised energy sources, such as passive solar heating, solar panels for heating water and generating electricity for individual buildings, and combined heat and power installations (CHP) in

local communities; and
• phasing out nuclear power, as a prime example of a centralised technology which is potentially disastrous for human health and the environment, imposes incalculable costs and risks on future generations, distracts attention from energy conservation and the scope for decentralised energy supply, and whose use in most developing countries would involve continuing economic dependence on the industrialised world.

Again, these changes will be encouraged by the changes in price structure brought about by a shift of taxation to fossil-fuel and nuclear energy at source, and the removal of perverse subsidies—such as the high level of UK government financial support over many years for nuclear energy R&D (research and development) contrasted with R&D on energy conservation, energy efficiency and solar power.

Resistance to raising the cost of energy is, of course, strong. The energy industries have forcefully resisted the proposed European carbon-energy tax, and agreement on an effective worldwide energy strategy at the 1997 Kyoto Conference on Climate Change. Furthermore, encouraging and empowering people to reduce energy consumption threatens conventional economic progress in a production-orientated world. Feminists see it also as threatening the masculine obsession with big new toys on the part of those whose influence still predominates in economic and technical affairs.

Work, Livelihoods And Social Cohesion

Tackling unemployment, poverty and social exclusion will be an essential aspect of transition to people-centred, sustainable development.

Conventional jobs will continue to be important, especially for the young, the untrained and the inexperienced. Policies should be changed which systematically encourage the replacement of labour by energy-intensive methods of production and distribution. But it is unrealistic to assume that conventional jobs can provide useful work and livelihoods for everyone, and questionable whether it is desirable that they should. It is becoming increasingly important to enable people to do useful work for themselves and one another, without having to depend on an employer to give them a job. In fact, much essential activity and useful work is unpaid. It includes parenting, household management, voluntary work, and active citizen participation in the neighbourhood and local community and in national and international affairs.

So, as with transport and energy, action is needed on the demand side as well as the supply side. As well as increasing the supply of jobs, we also need to reduce the demand for them by enabling people to get a livelihood and engage in useful activity without having to find an employer.

Again, shifting taxation away from employment and incomes on to the use of energy and resources and land-site values, and removing subsidies for energy-intensive processes, will alter price and cost structures in favour of increased employment. (Failure to tax site values raises land prices, thus making land unaffordable for people like potential small farmers and tradespeople who might otherwise work productively on it. It encourages landowners to hold land out of economic use in the hope of speculative capital gains as land values rise.) The Citizen's Income will provide both a platform on which people can build up paid work and an income base for useful unpaid work. Changes in education will also be needed, to prepare people not just for employment, but to manage their lives as adults and citizens, and as members of co-operative, community, neighbourhood and household groups.

Local Development
More self-reliant local development will play a key part in the transition to people-centred, environmentally sustainable ways of economic life. It will mean more use of local work and local resources (especially where these are now under-employed and under-used) to meet local needs (especially where these are now unmet). More cyclical, less linear patterns of local activity will reduce imports into and exports out of many local areas; increase the local recycling, reconditioning and re-use of local materials and equipment; and increase the recycling of local incomes and savings within the local economy. Increasing numbers of cities and rural areas are now exploring the practicalities for their own futures, under the Local Agenda 21 process initiated by the UNCED Earth Summit at Rio in 1992.[3]

For many years national governments, the European Commission

---

3. Two excellent reports, one for a metropolitan city and the other for a rural county, are *Creating A Sustainable London* (1996) and *Sustainable Gloucestershire* (1996).

and OECD have wrestled with the problems of economic crisis localities and regions, urban and rural. But these are systemic problems.
Transferring wealth from localities to the centre, and running down
local means of wealth creation and local capacity to meet local
needs, have been inherent features of conventional economic development. The revival of local economies has to be part of a transformation of the economic system as a whole. It is sometimes suggested that local communities should de-link unilaterally from the
national and global economy, and develop totally self-reliant local
economies (see Douthwaite, 1996). But unless mainstream economic institutions, policies, theories, values and attitudes change,
efforts to establish significant numbers of autonomous local
economies are unlikely to succeed, except perhaps in remote, self-
contained communities. More self-reliant local development should
be seen as a key part, but only one part, of a new multi-level
approach to economic activity worldwide. Localisation and a new
approach to globalisation together will mark the end of the 'wealth
of nations' era, and the emergence of a new decentralised one-
world economy.

Turning again to Box 1, a shift of taxation away from employment and incomes and on to energy use and pollution will encourage local production for local consumption by raising the costs of
centralised energy-intensive processes and long distance transport.
Removing subsidies and regulations that favour non-local production and non-local provision of services will do the same. By reducing land prices, site-value taxation will make land and housing more
affordable for local people. A Citizen's Income will make it easier for
local people to take up part-time work, and unpaid work, in the local
community.

To increase the circulation of money within local economies
where too little national currency circulates, in order to provide
means of exchange for purely local transactions, local government
authorities should be permitted to issue local currencies, and local
community groups should be encouraged to set up LETS. Local
banks and financial institutions should be encouraged, to enable
local people to invest their savings in the local economy. (These
points are taken up in Chapter 4.)

Other necessary measures will include planning policies that encourage local shops in villages, suburbs and small town centres, and discourage the monopolisation of local retailing and other trading by branches of businesses based elsewhere. Local indicators must be developed to monitor changes in local social, environmental and economic conditions, including the impacts of branches of outside organisations on local employment, local production, local money flows, and the local environment.

Technology

Supporters of people-centred, environmentally sustainable development are not Luddites—quite the reverse. New advanced technologies which conserve resources and reduce pollution, and which enable people, local communities and developing countries to become more self-reliant, will be crucial. They will contribute directly to the changes in farming and food, travel and transport, energy, work, and local economic life we have been discussing. Their development will make it possible to compete successfully in the growing world market for technologies of that kind.

The modern industrial world has favoured centralising, dependency-creating, unecological technologies. In the conventional production-orientated economy, whether business-centred or state-centred, it has rarely occurred to governments—and scientists, technologists and engineers—to develop technologies designed to help people become more self-reliant; and because producers have been able to externalise their environmental costs, the market has provided little incentive to develop resource-conserving, non-polluting technologies.

Technological innovation is a double-edged sword. Communication and computer technologies, for example, can be developed to give people decentralised power to communicate with one another by phone and fax and e-mail and through small decentralised newsletters and journals. (The use of faxes played a significant part in the popular movements that led to the break-up of the Soviet Union.) But communication and computer technologies can also be used for surveillance and manipulation, allowing the Big Brother organisations of business and government to keep track of where people are and what they are doing, and allowing transnational corporate press and broadcasting conglomerates to shape public opinion. Biotechnologies raise even more difficult problems. While special laws and regulations will continue to be needed to deal with some of those, restructuring the tax system and eliminating perverse subsidies (including subsidies for the wrong kinds of R&D), will help to stimulate demand for new, decentralised, ecological technologies.

Schumacher himself saw technology as 'the base', in contrast to laws, taxes, welfare, education, health services, etc. which he called 'the superstructure'. He said: "I know of no better way of changing the 'system' than by putting into the world a new type of technology— technologies by which small people can make themselves productive and relatively independent" (*This I Believe*, page 100). New humane and conserving technologies are certainly vital. But I suspect they will break through on a significant scale only as part of a larger transformation, including changes in taxes and laws.

Business

The ideological shift to 'free markets' and 'free trade' in the 1980s and 1990s has enlarged the freedom of large business corporations to skew the world's economic system in their own favour.

For example, intra-firm trade between the national components of transnational corporations (which constitutes about half of all international trade) is not free trade. Free trade does not operate in sectors of world trade such as food and agriculture, in which rich-country multinationals predominate. Nations have become dependent on the big business sector for sponsorship for sport, arts, culture and (to some extent) community projects. Local government relies on big businesses to provide finance for new local amenities in return for favourable planning treatment, e.g. permission to build new superstores that put local shops out of business. (This is known as 'planning gain'.) Governments compete against one another to attract inward investment by multinationals, by offering them bigger subsidies and tax breaks at the expense of their taxpayers. Backed by the governments of the most powerful nations, and having themselves become more powerful than many national governments, transnational corporations now "rule the world" (Korten, 1995).

It is not realistic to expect large business corporations to provide the driving force for the global transformation now needed. They compete in a predatory world economy in which shifting to equitable and sustainable behaviour would jeopardise their short-term survival and success, unless their competitors are compelled to do the same. That means changing the rules of the game and the scoring system, to maintain fair competition—'a level playing field'—and push more backward-looking as well as more forward-looking firms in the right direction. The rules of the game are laws and regulations; they must compel business to observe mandatory social and environmental standards. The scoring system is the structure of costs and prices in the economy; it must be changed to make socially and environmentally benign business activities financially attractive.

So again we come back to the same framework changes, including the restructuring of taxation. So far as subsidies are concerned, all perverse subsidies to business should be stopped as soon as possible. Over the longer term, the transition from a business-centred to a people-centred economy will involve phasing out subsidies to business altogether. The savings should help to finance the Citizen's Income so that citizens, not corporate managements, can decide how their money is spent.

These external financial changes in the business environment should be supplemented by internal changes to improve their accountability to their 'stakeholders'. In the short term, government should legislate for mandatory annual publication of social and environmental audits by businesses of a certain size and type, and should let public contracts only to businesses which comply satisfactorily. In the longer term, there may be a case for democratising the corporate structures of big business ownership and control, so that the rights (and obligations) of all the stakeholders (including future generations) are represented in their decision-making processes. Changes in company law to that effect will be necessary (Goyder, G., 1993).

Health, and Law And Order

We have mentioned the need to reduce the demand for travel and transport, energy and jobs, as well as improving their supply. The need to reduce demand is particularly clear in fields like health and law and order.

Health policies and health services today are mainly about responding to sickness and ill-health after they have occurred. Similarly, law-and-order policies and services (prisons, police, law courts, etc.) mainly deal with the after-effects of crime and disorderly behaviour. In other words, both provide remedial services, at the 'end-of-the-pipe'. Successful healthy public policies, which worked 'upstream' to create a healthier society, would reduce the demand for conventional health services. Successful law-and-order policies, which helped to create a more law-abiding society, would reduce the demand for police and prisons and law courts.

Sickness services and police and prisons will never be unnecessary—though it could be a useful exercise to spell out what the economy of such an imaginary Utopia might be like. But a healthier and more cohesive, more law-abiding society will be created by changes for the better in sectors like farming and food, transport, energy, employment and work, planning and housing, not by policies and professions primarily concerned with 'health' and 'law and order'.

Two conclusions emerge. First, the framework changes in Box 1 will help to create a healthier and more cohesive society, as well as change for the better in other sectors. Second, reducing demand for many types of goods and services will be an important feature of the transition to a people-centred, sustainable future. Might reducing conventional economic growth even be good for people and the Earth? Comparing the New Economic Foundation's Index of Sustainable Welfare with GDP from 1975 and 1996 suggests we should not rule this out (see New Economics Foundation, 1997).

An Interim Conclusion

Hitherto, public finance has been the jealously guarded territory of financial ministries and departments, like the Treasury in the UK. But its systemic influence on the economy as a whole makes it too important to remain the specialist preserve of finance experts. The measures summarised in Box 1 will encourage necessary change in many sectors of the economy. Activists in these various sectors should co-operate to get them brought in.[4] Chapter 3 discusses them further.

---

4. The Real World Coalition is a good example of such a collaborative initiative by a large group of NGOs—see Jacobs, M. (1996).

Chapter 3
SHARING THE VALUE
OF COMMON RESOURCES
Taxation And Public Expenditure

A Restructured Tax System and a Citizen's Income

"The earth shall become a common treasury to all, as it was first made and given to the sons of men." Gerrard Winstanley (1649)

Pressures are growing for a general restructuring of taxation and welfare benefits. At present they encourage inefficient use of resources—over-use of natural resources (including the environment's capacity to absorb pollution and waste), and under-use and under-development of human resources. By failing to discourage environmentally damaging activities, they fail to encourage innovation for sustainability and a larger share of the growing world market for environmental technologies and services. They discourage both employment and useful unpaid work like parenting. Means-tested benefits discourage saving, as well as the earning of income. They create poverty and unemployment traps which reinforce social exclusion and raise costs for education, health, and law and order. The cost of the welfare state is already at crisis level in many countries.

For the future, an ageing society will find it even more difficult to tax fewer people of working age on the fruits of their employment and enterprise in order to support a growing number of 'economically inactive' people. In the medium term at least, a competitive global economy will exert pressure for lower taxes on personal incomes and business profits in order to attract inward investment.

That is the context for the proposal to combine:

- ecotax reform (i.e. a shift of taxation away from employment, incomes and savings, on to resource-depleting and environmentally damaging activities),
- the further replacement of existing taxes by another resource tax—a tax on land site-values, and

- the introduction of a Citizen's Income.

This combination would be phased in over a period of years. It would embody a new social compact for a new era of equitable and sustainable development, in which full employment of the conventional kind, a welfare state of the conventional kind, and economic growth of the conventional kind, had become obsolete goals.

Ecotax Reform

Environmental taxes have been seen as pollution taxes, reflecting the 'polluter pays' principle. In economists' jargon, they would 'internalise' costs previously 'externalised' by polluters.

They are now coming to be seen more broadly as taxes on the use of natural resources—the capacity of the environment to absorb pollution and wastes being one such resource. Energy taxes, water charges, and traffic congestion charges are other resource taxes. The principle is that people should pay for the benefits they get from using 'commons' of all kinds, meaning resources and values created by nature or society and not by themselves. For example, in its 1995 Report the British Government Panel on Sustainable Development supported taxing people "on the value they subtract" rather than "the value they add".

Ecotax reform is concerned not just with ecotaxes themselves, but with how the revenue from them should be used. The European Commission's White Paper on Growth, Competitiveness, Employment of December 1993 proposed to use ecotax revenues to reduce taxes on employment. This approach has now been developed in many official and unofficial studies and reports, and has in some instances (as in the UK's landfill tax) been put into practice.

But there is a serious problem. If existing taxes on incomes, profits and savings are simply replaced with environmental and resource taxes on consumers, they will hit poorer people relatively harder than richer. Regardless of the taxes they replace, ecotaxes are bound to have this regressive effect if they are applied 'downstream' at the point of consumption. For example, value-added tax (VAT) on household energy hits poorer households harder than richer ones, because they do not have the money to pay the higher cost of the tax or to invest in greater energy efficiency; and similarly, fees and charges to reduce urban congestion will hurt small tradespeople who need to use their vehicles for their work, but will be painlessly absorbed by users of chauffeur-driven limousines. If ecotaxes are to replace existing taxes significantly, this problem will have to be solved. How?

First, ecotaxes should, as far as possible, be applied 'upstream'. A tax on fossil fuels and nuclear energy, collected at source and cascading down through the economy, will raise the cost of the energy content of all goods and services. This will have three advantages. It will reduce pollution, because pollution mostly arises from energy-intensive activities. It will be seen to be fair because, by raising costs for producers as well as prices for consumers of energy-intensive goods and services, it will clearly hit the salaries, dividends, capital appreciation, etc. of big producer interests and not just the pockets of small consumers. And it will be simpler administratively and easier to understand than a proliferation of separate ecotaxes on individual consumers and polluters.

Second, a tax on land will help to offset the regressive effect of ecotaxes. A site-value tax is a resource tax that is progressive. It is the rich, not the poor, who become rich from the value of land.

Third, the revenue from ecotaxes should be used progressively. A German study (DIW, 1994) concluded that, if part of the revenue from an energy tax were distributed to households as an ecobonus, the change would have positive economic and employment effects, and would reduce the net tax burden on low-income households. A Swiss study (von Weizsacker, 1994, p76) concluded that if the revenue from levying two Swiss francs per litre of petrol were distributed to all adults as an ecobonus, people driving less than 7,000 kilometres a year would benefit, while people driving more would lose.

So, could ecobonuses add up to a Citizen's Income? And could a Citizen's Income be financed from from resource tax revenues? These questions are discussed later in this chapter.

Site-Value Land Taxation

The proposal is to tax the annual rental site value of land. That does not include the value of developments carried out by the owner and his predecessors (which should not be taxed). It is the value of the land as provided by nature and as affected for better or worse by the activities and regulations of society. Estimates for Britain in 1990 suggest the relative size of these values (£bn) for various land uses: housing 66.4; commerce 19.0; public services 10.2; industry 9.3; farm, woodland and forest 2.4 (from David Richards, 1990).

This tax has attracted favourable comment from economists since Adam Smith. Ricardo (1817) pointed out that a "tax on rent would affect rent only; it would fall wholly on landlords and could not be shifted to any class of consumers". In 1879, in *Progress And Poverty*, the American economist Henry George showed that to shift the burden of taxation from production and exchange to the value of land would stimulate employment and the production of wealth; the selling price of land would fall; land speculation would receive its death-blow; and land monopolisation would no longer pay. Leading economists since then have agreed that the tax on economic rent is the most neutral and most efficient of all taxes, inducing no distortions and generating no loss of welfare (Fred Harrison in Ronald Banks, ed., 1989). Various political parties in Europe during the 20th century have included site-value taxation in their policies, and it provides a component of local taxation in a number of countries today. But mainstream policy analysts and economists in recent years have shown a strange lack of interest in it. Merely a case of professional groupthink? Or, as some suggest (Mason Gaffney and Fred Harrison, 1994) the result of an intellectual conspiracy originally inspired by landowning interests early this century?

Some past advocates of the site value tax have put people off by insisting that, as the 'single tax' needed to finance all public spending, it should replace all others. Today, its more forward-looking advocates present its claims as one resource tax among others. Their arguments for a system of public finance based on socialising (i.e. taxing) the rent of land and other natural resources, and privatising (i.e. not taxing) people's wages and savings, appear wholly convincing.

Citizen's Income (or Basic Income)

The proposal is to distribute a Citizen's Income (CI)—often known as a Basic Income—as a tax-free income paid by the state to every man, woman and child as a right of citizenship. It will be age-related, with more for adults than children and more for elderly people than working-age adults. CI for children will replace today's child benefit, and CI for the elderly will replace today's state pensions. There will be supplements for disability, housing benefits, and other exceptional circumstances. Otherwise CI will replace all existing benefits and tax allowances. The amount of a person's CI will be unaffected by their income or wealth, their work status, gender or marital status.

The idea of a basic income goes back to Thomas Paine in the 1790s and to the Fourierists and John Stuart Mill in the first half of the 19th century. In Britain in the 1920s, Major C.H. Douglas proposed Social Credit as a response to unemployment. More recently, support has come from distinguished economists, including Samuel Brittan and James Meade. Most contemporary CI supporters have assumed that CI would be financed out of income tax, but opinion within the CI movement is now shifting towards financing it from "sources reflecting a 'common endowment'".

Support for CI continues to grow, especially in Britain and Western Europe. A recent study (Clark, C. and Healy, J., 1997) showed that a full Citizen's Income could be introduced in Ireland over a period of three budgets. It would result in nobody receiving less than the poverty line of income; all unemployment and poverty traps being eliminated; and it always being worthwhile for an unemployed person to take up a job. The principle underlying the proposal was that "Nature and its resources are for the benefit of all".

Targeting or Universality?

At first sight, it seems more sensible and less costly to target benefits strictly to those who really need them, rather than to distribute them to everyone. But targeting involves means testing. There is no other way to establish need and eligibility. And means testing has serious disadvantages: it is experienced as demeaning and socially divisive; to avoid it, many people fail to take up benefits to which they are entitled; it tightens the unemployment and poverty traps, by reducing incentives to earn and save; and people who have earned and saved enough to disqualify themselves from means-tested benefits, feel resentment against those who have not—creating more social divisiveness.

The universality of a Citizen's Income avoids these disadvantages. But the total direct cost of CI to government will be much higher than the cost of selective benefits based on means-tested need; and it is argued that poor people should not be given an unearned income as a hand-out from the state.[1] However, these objections can be met by combining a CI with a restructured tax system, whereby the CI's value (or more) will be clawed back from better-off people via taxes on their use or monopolisation of common resources, and CI will be seen as everyone's share of the value of those resources.

The result will be doubly progressive. The CI will be progressive because the same amount of money is worth relatively more to poor people. The taxes will be progressive because richer people will pay more for the disproportionately large financial benefits they now enjoy (in terms of salaries, dividends and capital appreciation) from the ownership of land and the use of common resources.

Towards A New Social Compact
Part of the transition, then, to a people-centred, environmentally sustainable future will be a package of reforms based on:

- the introduction of taxes and charges on the use of common resources and values, particularly including energy and land;
- the reduction, and perhaps the eventual abolition, of taxes and charges on employment, incomes, profits, value added, and capital; and
- the introduction of a Citizen's Income, to which ecobonuses will contribute, paid to all citizens as of right in place of all tax reliefs and many existing welfare benefits.

The ecotax reform movement has been gathering strength in mainstream policy-making and academic research but still faces serious problems. The movements for site-value taxation and Citizen's Income are growing stronger but yet have to mobilise mainstream momentum. Over the next few years the potential synergies between the three will become clear. Beyond the practical arguments for treating them as a package, an integrating vision will emerge.

It will be a vision of a people-centred society—less employer-centred and state-centred than today's—which does not tax people for what they earn by their useful work and enterprise, by the value they

---

1. It is noticeable that the unearned incomes which rich and middle-income people derive from "enclosure of the commons" are seldom similarly questioned!

add, and by what they contribute to the common good; in which the amounts that people and organisations are required to pay to the public revenue are based on the value they subtract by their use or monopolisation of common resources; and in which all citizens are equally entitled to share in the annual revenue so raised, partly by way of services provided at public expense and partly by way of a Citizen's Income.

The citizens of such a society will be more equal with one another in esteem, capability and material conditions of life than now. They will find it easier to get paid work, but they will no longer be as dependent as they are now on employers to provide them with incomes and organise work for them. The modern-age class division between employers and employees will fade—as the old master/slave and lord/serf relationships of ancient and medieval societies have faded. It will be normal for people to work for themselves and one another. It will become an aim in many fields of policy to enable people to manage their own working lives.

The social compact of the employment age is now breaking down. The time is passing when the great majority of citizens, excluded from access to land and other means of production and from their share of common resources and values, could nevertheless depend on employers to provide them with adequate incomes in exchange for work, and on the state for special benefit payments to see them through exceptional periods of unemployment. A new social compact will encourage all citizens to take greater responsibility for themselves and their contribution to society. In exchange, it will recognise their right to share in the value of the 'commons', enabling them to become less dependent than they are today on big business and big finance, on employers, and on officials of the state.

Public Expenditure Programmes

"In prehistoric times there might have been some parliamentary control over public expenditure, but there certainly has not been in my parliamentary experience."—Arthur Balfour, 1905.

The need to transform the major part of welfare spending into a Citizen's Income has been discussed. What about the rest of public spending?

Perverse Subsidies and the Market Economy
The need to remove perverse subsidies in many areas of the economy was noted in Chapter 2. The UK Government's Panel on Sustainable Development has estimated (January 1997) the total value of environmentally damaging subsidies in Britain at more than £20 billion a year. Estimates of the worldwide value of perverse subsidies range between $500bn (Wuppertal 1997) and $1,500bn (Myers 1998). Perverse subsidies are worse than merely a waste of citizens' money: they skew the price structure of the economy in favour of socially and environmentally undesirable activities, as do perverse taxes.

But how are subsidies defined? What do they include? In addition to subsidies in the narrow sense, there are other forms of de facto subsidisation which artificially improve the competitive position of some products and activities against others by influencing market prices in their favour. Examples include: discriminatory taxes, such as the de facto subsidy to energy consumption due to its lower rate of Value Added Tax than on energy-saving equipments; higher public spending on R & D in one field than in competing fields, as on nuclear power against energy efficiency and energy conservation; higher public spending on one type of transport infrastructure than on others, such as road against rail; and the de facto subsidy given by today's tax system to energy-intensive production and distribution, against employment and useful unpaid work.

The point is that the whole array of public spending programmes and taxes existing at any one time, together with the non-existence of public spending and taxation on other things, moves market prices in favour of certain kinds of activities against others. As we have said, some such framework has to exist. It should be designed to encourage social equity, environmental sustainability, and economic efficiency and enterprise, and to minimise the need for ad hoc government interventions in the workings of the market.

Democratic control over the nature of this framework and its effects is virtually non-existent. At the least, parliaments should insist on governments publishing a comprehensive annual statement on the social and environmental impacts of subsidies provided under each spending programme. If representatives of NGOs and pressure groups were included in the teams drawing up these statements, their effectiveness would be enhanced.

Should There Be Any Subsidies At All?

Should subsidies be given to activities and products that positively contribute to people-centred sustainable development?

In the short term there is probably a case for this. For example, the favourable tax treatment recently introduced in the Netherlands for environmental investment funds may encourage some savers to consider green investments sooner than they would otherwise have done, and may help to stimulate banks and other financial concerns to provide environmental investment services. As a temporary measure, it and other comparable subsidies, for example to support conversions to organic farming, may serve a useful purpose.

But, if introduced at all, such subsidies should be seen as strictly temporary. In each case the same questions need to be asked: What are the distortions in the economy that make it necessary to subsidise this desirable activity? How can those distortions be removed? In almost every case the answer will be that price distortions arising from perverse subsidies or perverse taxes bias the economy against the activities desired. It is better to remove existing perverse taxes and subsidies than to introduce additional subsidies to counteract their effects. Environmental investment and organic farming, for example, will both get a bigger boost from ecotax reform than from subsidies.

In today's business-centred, employer-centred, government-centred economy, the use of public funds to encourage the provision of goods and services and jobs by businesses, employers and government rather than by citizens for themselves and one another, may be understandable. But, in a more people-centred economy that offers citizens greater freedom of choice and enables them to take more responsibility for themselves and one another, this use of public funds will be increasingly questioned. It will become obvious that much existing expenditure on government programmes would more appropriately finance a Citizen's Income.

Lower Total Public Spending?

That is one reason to look for a reduction in conventional public spending programmes over the coming years. There is another.

As we said in Chapter 2, a high proportion of public expenditure now is remedial. It deals with the after-effects of crime, unemployment, social exclusion, ill-health, environmental damage, humanitarian disasters, breakdowns of law and order, and so on. Reorientation of public policy and public spending towards the creation of conditions leading to less crime, social exclusion, ill-health, environmental damage, and so on is a high priority.

To take one of many possible examples, there is growing evidence that diets that are deficient in certain vitamins and trace elements and containing certain additives and other chemical substances, are a significant cause of attention deficit and hyperactivity in children, which can develop into anti-social and criminal behaviour as they grow older. But few professionals in the police, prisons and other law-and-order services, in the education and employment services, in the medical and health (i.e. sickness) services, or in the drug companies, are interested. How a dietary approach might help such children, their families and society in terms of improved quality of life, improved education, improved economic capacities and improved life prospects, and what existing costs it might save, is still largely unexplored.

In general, a new approach to public spending is needed, to identify possibilities for re-orientating it toward prevention instead of cure. But, to be realistic, the professions which have grown up in remedial fields of public service, and the bureaucracies and commercial interests which support them, are likely to be unenthusiastic. How many health practitioners and health officials, for example, can we expect to contribute to health-creating innovations in transport, energy, employment, planning, taxation, welfare benefits, or food and farming? The initiative to reorientate public policy from cure to prevention will have to come mainly from outside today's remedial professions.

As the changes in taxes, benefits and public spending proposed here are phased in over the years, they will help people and localities to meet for themselves many needs now met by government programmes. This will bring phased reductions in total public spending, which will allow corresponding reductions in the overall burden of taxation. So we should not worry too much that resource and pollution taxes may be so effective in reducing resource use and pollution that the revenue they are able to raise will eventually decline.

Chapter 4

MONEY & FINANCE

"If money be not thy servant, it will be thy master." Pierre Charron (1601)

Most of the sectoral changes outlined in Chapter 2 have been well worked through by NGOs, professional experts and others in recent years. The changes they call for in the sphere of public finance, discussed in Chapter 3, are fairly straightforward. Not everyone agrees with them; they will have to be campaigned for. But it is not too difficult to see how governments and government agencies could introduce them, given the political will.

But a people-centred, environmentally sustainable economy will also involve changes in the way the actual money and finance system works. Some specific innovations, such as LETS, microcredit, local financial institutions and ethical (social and green) investment, have become part of the new economics agenda. But money is conceptually slippery. It is clouded in professional mystery. It is difficult for policy makers in other fields, and for NGOs, to get to grips with it. Working out a strategy for change, and mobilising support for it, is a top priority.

Damaging Effects
Today's money and finance system is unfair, ecologically destructive, and economically inefficient. It systematically transfers resources from poor to rich. The money-must-grow imperative drives production (and thus consumption) to higher than necessary levels. It skews economic effort towards making money out of money, and against providing real goods and services.

Transfer of Resources from Poor to Rich
The transfer of resources from poor people to rich people, from poor places to rich places, and from poor countries to rich countries by the money and finance system is systematic. No-one actually decides from time to time that this is a desired policy goal. It compels

poor people and countries, and encourages rich ones, to consume resources and create pollution and waste faster than they would otherwise do. The poor have to do it to survive. The affluent, for whom economic survival offers no problem, enjoy the luxury to do it both in their leisure activities and in pursuit of further financial growth and success.

One cause of the transfer of wealth from poor people to rich is the way interest payments and receipts work through the economy. Dividing the population into ten sections of equal size, a German study (Kennedy 1995) suggested that the effect of interest is that the richest section receives far more than it pays, the second richest receives a little more, and the other eight receive less. The result is a substantial transfer of money from the poorer majority to the rich minority.

The transfer of money from poorer to richer localities takes place through the automatic workings of the national and international banking and financial networks. As poorer localities offer few attractive investment opportunities, savings from them are channelled into investments in richer parts of the country or richer parts of the world which offer better returns. This reflects the service that the banking and financial system is expected to provide for savers and investors, and it is how it expects to make profits for itself. The same principle leads to the transfer of financial resources from poorer to richer countries.

Third World debt in the 1980s and 1990s illustrates some of the causes and effects of the systematic transfer of wealth from poorer to richer countries. International interest rates rose and so did the cost of imported knowhow and technologies, while international commodity prices fell. Through no fault of their own, indebted Third World countries found themselves faced with escalating debts, resulting from higher interest rates and import prices to be paid and reduced foreign exchange earnings to pay them.[1] The response of the International Monetary Fund and the World Bank was to prescribe development that placed even greater emphasis on the export of commodities at low world prices.

---

1.   Out of the $1,200 billion owed by the Third World to the First World in 1990, only $400bn constituted the original borrowing. The rest consisted of accrued interest and capital liabilities (Brown, M.B., 1993, p43).

The immediate need, as the Jubilee 2000 Campaign insists, is to cancel the unrepayable debts of the poorest countries as a millennial commitment to equitable and sustainable world development. In the longer term, the loan needs of Third World countries should be reduced by paying them annual 'rental' payments in compensation for the disproportionately large use of world resources by the industrialised countries—see Chapter 5.

Money Must Grow [2]

The money-must-grow imperative is ecologically destructive. National Income must grow, corporate profits and stockmarket values must grow, financial institutions want the money supply and consumer credit to grow, and individuals want their incomes and financial assets to grow. This money-must-grow compulsion drives economic activity—production and therefore consumption—to higher levels than would otherwise be needed. For example, interest and the discount rate encourage rapid exploitation of resources. Converting resources into a financial profit now and investing the profit, yields a financial return; whereas leaving the resources in the ground or the sea yields no return until they are extracted.

The money-must-grow imperative also results in a massive worldwide diversion of effort away from providing useful goods and services, into making money out of money. At least 95% of the billions of dollars transferred daily around the world are for purely financial transactions, unlinked to transactions in the real economy.

Signs Of A Paradigm Shift

People are increasingly experiencing the workings of the money, banking and finance system as unreal, incomprehensible, unaccountable, irresponsible, exploitative and out of control. Why should they lose their houses and their jobs as a result of financial decisions taken in distant parts of the world? Why should the national and international money and finance system involve the systematic transfer of wealth from poor people to rich people, and from poor countries to rich countries? Why should someone in Singapore be able to gamble on the Tokyo stock exchange and bring about the

---

2. Hoogendijk, W. (1991 and subsequent papers) explores this problem.

collapse of a bank in London? Why, when taking out a pension, should people have had to rely on advice corrupted by the self-interest of the advisers? Why do young people trading derivatives in the City of London get annual bonuses larger than the whole annual budgets of primary schools? Do we have to have a money and financial system that works like this? Even the financier George Soros has said ('Capital Crimes', *Atlantic Monthly*, January 1997) that "the untrammelled intensification of laisser-faire capitalism and the extension of market values into all areas of life is endangering our open and democratic society. The main enemy of the open society, I believe, is no longer the communist but the capitalist threat".

This growing awareness of today's failings is accompanied by growing awareness of tomorrow's possibilities. Over the centuries money has evolved from concrete to abstract—from metal bars and coins, to paper notes and cheques, and now to numbers electronically stored in computer files and transmitted electronically between them. As this stage has arrived—with the transformation of the great majority of monetary and financial assets and liabilities into entries in computerised accounts, and of the great majority of monetary and financial transactions into electronic messages that debit and credit the accounts of payer and payee—our collective understanding of money and its role in economic life is reaching a watershed. It is becoming increasingly apparent that the money and finance system is basically an information system—an accounting system (or scoring system) that indicates the claims we are entitled to make on one another for goods and services now and in the future, and enables us to trade one type of claim (e.g. money in a bank account) for another type of claim (e.g. an insurance policy or a shareholding in a business). The future role of the internet in this monetary scoring and information system is already widely discussed.

In the next few decades, questions about the nature and functions of money will become more pressing. What is money, and what is it for? Should it reflect objective values, or should it be recognised as just a practical device to facilitate exchanges between people? Who does the money system belong to, and to whom should those who manage it be accountable? Why does it now work so badly?

This Briefing cannot go into these questions in depth. But as the post-modern transition proceeds and the extent to which we create our own pluralistic realities becomes more widely understood, the money and finance system will increasingly be understood to be a device which can be designed and developed by people for people's purposes. The idea that there must be only one kind of money at national level or even European or eventually even global level—a single currency that everyone should be compelled to use—will come to seem archaic. The primitive notion that monetary and banking experts—like a priesthood or scientific élite whose arcane methods people cannot hope to understand—should be entrusted with the task of keeping money values in line with mysteriously existing numerical realities out there, will increasingly be recognised as fraudulent. It will be understood that money has no intrinsic value, and need have none. It simply needs to work well for the task that people need it for. In this context, Local Exchange Trading Systems (LETS), though still marginal in practice, embody a potentially important model for the future—the model of a money system as essentially something we can create for ourselves to facilitate exchanges between us.

A Single or Multiple Currency System?

Eleven West European nations now seem set to give up their national currencies for a single European currency—the euro—under European Monetary Union (EMU).

Compelling everyone to use a particular currency is in line with the well-established historical impulse to centralise economic power and decision making. As Jane Jacobs (1986) said, "Today we take it for granted that the elimination of multitudinous currencies in favor of fewer national or imperial currencies represents economic progress and promotes the stability of economic life. But this conventional belief is still worth questioning... National or imperial currencies give faulty or destructive feedback to city economies and this in turn leads to profound structural flaws in those economies, some of which cannot be overcome, however hard we try".

Rural local economies, too, confront the same problem. When any local economy, urban or rural, has to depend on national (or supranational) currencies as the basis for economic activity within its own local boundaries, declining local competitiveness in the larger economy will result in too little money coming into local circulation even to support entirely local transactions between local people. Local unemployment then rises, local land and other physical assets lie unused, and local needs remain unmet—because not enough money circulates locally as a local medium of exchange. The monetary policies and demand management policies appropriate for a national (or continental) economy at any particular time are bound to be inappropriate for many of the local (or national) economies within it. More flexibility is needed.

Significant pointers to the future include a growing number of local currencies or quasi-currencies (including LETS). A great deal of useful literature now exists on local currencies, including many in the USA and other countries today, as well as those in Austria in the 1930s which successfully reduced local unemployment before being suppressed by the Austrian government and central bank. (See Greco 1994, Douthwaite 1996, and the references they quote).

It would be logical to suppose that the simultaneous shift towards greater globalisation and greater localisation of economic life would be accompanied by the emergence of both supranational and local currencies alongside national currencies. This would reflect the subsidiarity principle. It would have implied organic development towards a multi-level European system of currencies, with

• a new common (not single) European currency,
• existing national currencies,
• optional new local currencies, quasi-currencies and media of exchange, issued by such local government authorities as chose to issue them, and
• optional neighbourhood and community quasi-currencies and media of exchange, on the lines of LETS.

No-one can tell how EMU will work out in practice. But, as things now stand, Britain, Denmark, Greece and Sweden will be the only EU member states whose citizens will be entitled to continue using their own national currencies, while being able to arrange to use the euro for particular transactions when more convenient. In practice, they will enjoy the freedom of choice offered by a multiple currency system. Local government authorities and local neighbourhood and community groups should also have the option to introduce their own means of exchange if they think it necessary. Computerised bank systems can easily handle multiple currency accounts and provide other multi-currency services for their customers.

"Evaluating the implications of multiple and, particularly, complementary currency systems... is practically a virgin academic field" (Lietaer 1996). Monetary authorities and monetary economists have never seriously studied how a multi-level currency system would work. It is high time to put this right.

Interest, Debt and Electronic Money

So the effects of interest include transferring money from poor to rich, accelerating resource extraction and environmental damage, and diverting effort to making money out of money. But there are other questions about interest too.

• Why has the process of issuing new money into the economy (i.e. credit creation) been delegated by governments to the banks, allowing them to profit from issuing it in the form of interest-bearing loans to their customers? Should governments not issue it directly themselves, as a component of a Citizen's Income?

• Would it be desirable and possible to limit the role of interest more drastically than that, for example by converting debt into equity throughout the economy? This would be in line with Islamic teaching, and with earlier Christian teaching, that usury is a sin. Although the practical complications would make this a goal for the longer term, there are strong arguments for exploring it—the extent to which economic life worldwide now depends on ever-rising debt, the danger of economic collapse this entails, and the economic power now enjoyed by those who make money out of money rather than out of risk-bearing participation in useful enterprises. (Tomlinson 1993 and Kennedy 1994 provide good starting points.)

• May there be a role for negative interest rates? These were proposed early this century by Silvio Gesell (from whom Keynes said the future would learn more than from Marx). The Austrian local currency experiments of the 1930s required each currency note to be revalidated every month by attaching a special stamp costing 2% of its value. This stimulated the local economy by encouraging people to spend, not hoard, the local money. Could other liquid financial assets, like current account bank balances, be subject to negative interest rates? And would that be a good idea?

These questions must be explored in the context of deregulation and electronic money. Increasing numbers of retailers will continue to launch their own credit cards, loyalty cards and other forms of credit. Combined with developments in electronic and plastic money, including rechargeable cash cards and money transmission over the internet, this will mean radical change. It may continue to be unplanned and piecemeal. But, as Hayek (1978) foresaw, it is possible that a free money movement comparable to the 19th-century free trade movement may emerge. Arguing that government monopoly of money has been the cause of inflation, financial instability, undisciplined public expenditure and economic nationalism, Hayek suggested its replacement by competition in currency supplied by private issuers. He also foresaw that "it will be through the credit card rather than through any kind of circulating token money that the government monopoly of the issue of money will be broken".

Financial Institutions

The shift to a people-centred, ecologically sustainable economic system will require a corresponding shift in the services offered by conventional financial institutions, and the further development of new financial institutions. The latter include ethical, green and social banks, investment funds and advisory services; and local development banks, microcredit banks, credit unions and other grass-roots people's banks which provide credit for people and localities unable to get it from conventional financial institutions.

The numbers of people interested in ethical investment will almost certainly continue to grow. Shifting taxation away from employment, incomes and business profits on to the use of energy, resources and pollution, and removing perverse subsidies, will increase the financial attractions of investing in people-centred, environmentally benign enterprises. So will making it mandatory for businesses to publish social and environmental audits, or allowing only businesses that publish them to bid for government contracts. In addition, as mentioned in Chapter 3, there may be a case for temporary subsidies or tax breaks for green and social investing.

Various types of community banks have been growing in numbers in North America and Europe and in countries of the South in recent years. They are set up to provide loans and other financial services to localities or groups of people (e.g. poor self-employed women in countries of the South) who are not served by conventional financial institutions. They include community development banks, like the Aston Reinvestment Trust in Birmingham and the South Shore Bank in Chicago; community development loan funds, which provide loans primarily for co-operatives, community businesses and other social-economy enterprises; credit unions; and microloan or micro-credit banks like the Grameen Bank in Bangladesh, which help small mutual-support groups of (mainly) women to save and borrow small amounts of money to enable them to start or expand their own small enterprises. These local banking and microcredit institutions will play a key part in enabling many people now unemployed to generate incomes for themselves and others, in more self-reliant local economies. Public policy should support them.

But this, by itself, will not transform the mainstream money system. Working out a strategy to transform it, and mobilising support for doing so, are top priorities. This is one of the most creative and crucial tasks facing the new economics movement.

Chapter 5

THE GLOBAL ECONOMY

"I sympathise, therefore, with those who would minimise, rather than with those who would maximise, economic entanglement between nations. Ideas, knowledge, art, hospitality, travel—these are the things which should of their nature be international. But let goods be home-spun whenever it is reasonably and conveniently possible; and, above all, let finance be primarily national." J.M. Keynes (1933)

The Context

The shift to a people-centred and environmentally sustainable world economic system will involve reversing central features of international economic development today, including the relatively higher rate of growth of international trade and financial flows than of economic output, and the growing dominance of business corporations in world economic governance. Higher costs of centralised energy-intensive production and long-distance transportation, arising from global taxation on global pollution and the use of global resources (see below) will help. But more effective and more democratic global institutions and policies will be needed too.

The world community will have to act on the following lines.

• The rich North will have to shift to a new conserving and empowering development path, as outlined in earlier chapters. This will involve more efficient use of a smaller share of the world's natural resources (which we now overuse), and more efficient use of our human resources (which we now underemploy and underdevelop).
• The countries of the South and the former Soviet bloc will also have to switch to this conserving and empowering development path. In our own self-interest the North must help these countries to do so.
• Today's global patterns of trade, investment and aid will have to change. So will existing ways of regulating them. The institutions of global economic governance will have to be brought under more democratic control. At present the World Bank, International Monetary Fund (IMF) and World Trade Organisation (WTO) do not

represent the majority of the world's peoples and do not have their confidence.[1]

NGOs and citizens' movements from both North and South will have to play an even more effective part in this change of direction in world development than they are playing already.

National Policies

National policies and programmes on export promotion, outward investment, aid and technology transfer, and trade, may have positive or negative effects on people-centred and ecologically sustainable development in other countries.

A government seriously committed to encouraging that kind of development in other countries will examine the effects of its support for arms exports. In general, governments should be pressed to publish systematic reviews of the extent to which their export promotion, outward investment, aid, technology transfer, and trade policies could be reorientated towards supporting equitable and sustainable development in other countries—for example, by supporting "fair trade".

A similar approach is needed at European level too. The Common Agricultural Policy should aim to promote food security in the South as well as in Europe. At present the EU's economic relations with the South are self-contradictory. The EU protects the interests of Southern countries by trade agreements, but at the same time damages them by import restrictions and export subsidies in support of its own trade interests (Sachs 1998, p217).

Global Policies And Institutions

In its existing form the UN system does not provide effective support for equitable and sustainable global development. And, because the World Bank, IMF and GATT/WTO (or whatever successor institutions take their place) will play such a key role in the 21st century, their present policies and position in the UN system must be changed.

---

1. The WTO was set up as the successor to GATT, "to implement the Uruguay Round, provide a forum for negotiation, administer the new mechanisms for dispute settlement and trade policy review, and co-ordinate with the IMF and World Bank for greater coherence in global policy making" (Commission on Global Governance, 1995, p168).

Reflecting orthodox economic principles and conventional economic philosophy, their bias towards development based on externally financed mega-projects, export-led growth and "free" trade, has reinforced the economic vulnerability of many countries in the South and has resulted in widespread poverty and environmental degradation.

Trade

"The highly integrated global economy of the 1990s, dominated by the activities of a few hundred transnational corporations, bears little relation to the economic configuration of the post-war 1940s in which the GATT rules were conceived, nor to the models of perfect competition which justified their emphasis on free trade. All but the most committed proponents of the free market recognise that efficient markets need effective government frameworks. Yet such a framework at the international level does not exist" (Ekins, 1993).

One-time World Bank economists Daly and Goodland (in a personal capacity, 1993) showed that unregulated free trade damages the environment and the development prospects of poorer countries. Daly and Cobb (1989) and Ekins (1995) have also shown that the classical 'comparative advantage' argument in support of unregulated free trade only applies in special hypothetical conditions which do not now exist (if they ever did). In recent years rising hostility to free trade has included strenuous opposition to the North American Free Trade Area (NAFTA), and currently to the proposed Multilateral Agreement on Investment which would allow multinationals to contest social and environmental laws. There have been many calls for a 'new protectionism' (e.g. Lang and Hines, 1993).

But experience shows that unilateral protectionist policies usually operate in favour of old established national monopolies and power groups. That damages the interests of the protectionist nation, as well as triggering tit-for-tat responses from other countries. An international framework of regulation is needed that will give all nations the same degree of trading freedom, while encouraging types of trade that contribute to self-reliant, sustainable development (see Commission on Global Governance, 1995, p170.)

The fair trading movement enables ethical consumers in the North to support small producers in the South. Backing has come from charities and NGOs concerned with Third World development, such as Oxfam, CIIR (Catholic Institute for International Relations) and Christian Aid. As they have developed methods of monitoring the social and environmental performance of producer organisations, they have been able to help—and persuade—large commercial companies to monitor their suppliers and contractors in the South (NEF/CIIR 1997). Fair trading should be actively supported by governments and the WTO.

Finance
Immediately, as a sign of millennial commitment to a global strategy for equitable development, the unrepayable debts of the poorest countries should be cancelled—see *Transfer of Resources from Poor to Rich* in Chapter 4. Longer-term changes, e.g. in the context of global taxation (below), must ensure that poor countries never again experience a debt crisis on the scale of the last twenty years.

Global Taxation
"A start must be made in establishing schemes of financing of global purposes, including charges for the use of global resources such as flight lanes, sea lanes, and ocean fishing areas, and the collection of global revenues agreed globally and implemented by treaty... It is time for the evolution of a consensus on the concept of global taxation for servicing the needs of the global neighbourhood" (Commission on Global Governance, 1995, p344). It would be reasonable to base the new global taxes on the use each nation makes of 'global commons', following the principle for national taxation discussed under Ecotax Reform in Chapter 3.

The following would be possible taxes of this kind (see Bezanson and Mendez in Cleveland, H. et al, 1995):

• taxes and charges on use of international resources such as ocean fishing, sea-bed mining, sea lanes, flight lanes, outer space, and the electro-magnetic spectrum;
• taxes and charges on activities that pollute and damage the global environment, or that cause hazards across (or outside) national boundaries, such as emissions of CO_2 and CFCs, oil spills, dumping wastes at sea, and other forms of marine and air pollution;
• a tax on military expenditures and the arms trade;
• a more general tax on world trade, designed both to raise inter-

national revenue and also to give a uniform worldwide incentive to greater national economic self-reliance; and

* a uniform tax on international currency exchange transactions.[2]

The revenue would accrue to a new global fund at UN level. Some of it could be distributed to all nations according to the size of their populations, reflecting the right of every person in the world to a 'global citizen's income' based on an equal share of the value of global resources. The rest of the revenue could finance UN expenditures, including international peace-keeping programmes.

This approach would encourage sustainable development worldwide; it would generate a much needed source of revenue for the UN; it would provide substantial financial transfers to developing countries by right and without strings, as 'rent' payments reflecting the disproportionate use of world resources by the rich countries; it would help to liberate developing countries from their present dependence on aid, foreign loans and rich-country-dominated institutions like the World Bank and the International Monetary Fund; and it would reduce the risk of another Third World debt crisis.

Towards A Global Currency?
The Commission on Global Governance (1995, p181) reported that the causes of instability in the international monetary and financial system include the globalisation of private financial markets, huge international financial flows which far exceed trade in their impacts on currency markets, the fact that the IMF's reserve currency—Special Drawing Rights (SDRs)—currently accounts for only a very minor part of world liquidity, and the fact that "the United States has the unique luxury of being able to borrow its own currency abroad and then devalue its repayment obligations". The Commission concluded that "there are important tasks to be performed by the IMF or any other custodian of the international financial system, and these are growing in urgency" (ibid, p183).

A *de facto* global currency has been in existence for a very long time. Under British and then American world economic supremacy in

---

2. This is known as a Tobin tax after James Tobin, the Nobel prize-winning economist who proposed it. It could serve a number of different purposes: to raise revenue; to discourage currency speculation; and, by building a cost threshold for imports and exports, to encourage national economic self-reliance.

the 19th and 20th centuries it has been sterling and then the dollar. A more democratic world economic system for the 21st century will demand a more democratic arrangement. One possibility would be to develop SDRs, initially as a world unit of account for use by the UN and others (e.g. transnational corporations) who found it convenient. In time this might evolve into a common (but not a single!) world currency. SDRs might be issued annually as a per capita distribution to national governments, either in the form of credits to developing countries (through the World Bank) for development aid, or to all countries (by an embryonic world central bank combining the existing functions of the IMF and the Bank for International Settlements). But, whatever form it takes, the development of a less imperialistic global monetary system will be a necessary part of the shift to a sustainable, people-centred world economy.

Restructuring Global Institutions

The tasks of the institutions of global economic governance set up after the 2nd World War have changed since 1945. They need to be restructured. Some key requirements are shown in Box 4.

BOX 4: Institutions of Global Economic Governance

• The UN must develop an effective capacity to agree and carry through a global strategy for equitable and sustainable development worldwide.

• The Group of Seven (now Eight, with Russia's inclusion) richest industrial nations must be replaced by a more representative World Economic Council.

• Closer co-ordination between the UN system and the Bretton Woods institutions is absolutely essential. In 1990 two recently retired top-level UN officials, Sir Brian Urquhart and the late Erskine Childers, doubted whether the UN's tasks would ever be carried out effectively "until the work of the IMF, the World Bank and the GATT is conducted in harmony and co-operation with the rest of the UN system". The 1995 Commission on Global Governance agreed.

• A Second Assembly representing the peoples of the world must be set up as a counterweight to the government representatives in the General Assembly and the Bretton Woods institutions.

We cannot go into these and other necessary changes here. But they present an important challenge for coalitions of NGOs and citizens' groups campaigning internationally. In the economic sphere, world leaders have never taken seriously their declaration at the 1990 Economic Summit in Houston that the 1990s would be "the Decade of Democracy". The comparative failure of UNCED in 1992, and the comparative failure to follow it up since then, illustrate the need for more effective global institutions. To be effective, they must be more democratic. If they are to negotiate and manage 'our common future', they must enjoy the confidence of the South as well as the North.

Conclusion

We now live in a one-world community. We share the problems of a single global economy. Few of the world's six billion people could withdraw from it into isolated local communities, even if they wanted to. But this does not mean the global economy should work as it works today. Historians in the 22nd century will look back in astonishment that people living now were brainwashed into believing the only way to gain a satisfactory livelihood was to compete with people on the far side of the world to produce and sell products most of which were not strictly necessary for a decent life.

A transformed economic system must empower and encourage people, communities and nations to take more control over their own economic destinies, to become more economically self-reliant, and to live in ways that are environmentally benign. The great majority of NGOs and citizens' movements are committed to people-centred development, and against development that is big-business-centred or state-centred. Their aim over the next few decades must be to reverse today's economic priorities and restructure economic institutions.

Personal and local community wellbeing must become paramount. National and transnational corporations, and national governments and international bodies like the World Bank and IMF, must take a supporting role. That way, and only that way, shall we transform the world's economic life, as if people and the Earth both matter.

SOME ORGANISATIONS & GROUPS

Chapter 1: Transforming The System
Two organisations offer a wide coverage:

New Economics Foundation, 1st Floor, Vine Court, 112-116 Whitechapel Road, London E1 1JE (Ed Mayo). Quarterly magazine. Current programmes include: community economic development; new economic indicators; social auditing and codes of conduct for business; value-based organisations; sustainable consumption; social entrepreneurs; and education for a new economics.

Sustainable Economy Unit, Forum for the Future, 227a City Road, London EC1V 1JT (Paul Ekins). Identifies ten strategic issues: greening the national accounts; implementing ecological tax reform; harnessing trade to sustainable development; linking sustainability, work and the welfare state; restructuring transport; reforming support for agriculture; developing solar power and energy efficiency; promoting a green industrial strategy; strengthening the local economy as an aspect of Local Agenda 21; and promoting environmental investment.

Others include:
Friends of the Earth (Sustainable Development Unit), 26-28 Underwood Street, London N1 7JQ (Duncan McLaren).
Green Alliance, 49 Wellington Street, London WC2E 7BN (Peter Madden).
Institute of Noetic Sciences, 475 Gate Five Road, Suite 300, Sausalito, CA 94965, USA (Thomas J. Hurley).
People-Centred Development Forum, 10588 NE Byron Drive, Bainbridge Island, WA 98110, USA (David Korten).
Real World Coalition, c/o Town and Country Planning Association, 17 Carlton House Terrace, London SW1Y 5AS.
Wuppertal Institute (for Climate, Environment and Energy), PO Box 100408, D-42004 Wuppertal, Germany (Ernst U. von Weizsacker).
WWF Europe, 36 Avenue de Tervuren B12, B-1040 Brussels (Tony Long).

Chapter 2: A Common Pattern
Farming and Food
SAFE (Sustainable Agriculture, Food and Environment) Alliance, 94 White Lion Street, London N1 9PF (Vicki Hird).
Soil Association, Bristol House, 40-56 Victoria Street, Bristol BS1 6BY (Patrick Holden).

Travel and Transport
Pedestrians' Association, 126 Aldersgate, London EC1 (Ben Plowden).
Sustrans, 35 King Street, Bristol BS1 4DZ (John Grimshaw).
Transport 2000, 10 Melton Street, London NW1 2EJ (Stephen Joseph).

Energy
Association for the Conservation of Energy, Westgate House, Prebend Street, London NW1 8PT (Andrew Warren).
Rocky Mountain Institute, 1739 Snowmass Creek Road, Snowmass, CO 81654, USA (Amory Lovins).

Work, Livelihoods and Social Cohesion
Europe 99, 21 Bd de Grenelle, 75015 Paris (Valerie Peugeot).
Justice Office, Conference of Religious of Ireland (CORI), Tabor House, Milltown Park, Dublin 6 (Fr. Sean Healy).

Local Development
Associacao IN LOCO, Apartado 603, 8000 Faro, Portugal (Alberto Melo).
European Network for Economic Self-Help and Local Development, Berlin Technical University, Franklinstrasse 28/29, D-10587 Berlin, Germany (Karl Birkholzer).
Sustainable London Trust, 7 Chamberlain Street, London NW1 8XB (John Jopling).
Sustainable Gloucestershire, Vision 21, 16 Portland Street, Cheltenham, Glos GL52 2PB (Lindsey Colbourne).

Technology
Intermediate Technology Development Group (ITDG), Schumacher Centre for Technology & Development, Bourton Hall, Bourton-on-Dunsmore, Warwicks CV23 9QZ (Catherine Budgett-Meakin).

Business
Centre for Tomorrow's Company, Royal Society of Arts, 8 John Adam Street, London WC2N 6EZ (Mark Goyder).
Institute of Social and Ethical Accountability, 1st Floor, Vine Court, 112-116 Whitechapel Road, London E1 1JE.
New Academy of Business, 3-4 Albion Place, Galena Road, London W6 0LT.

Chapter 3: Taxation and Public Spending
Ecotax Reform (see also under Chapter 1 above.)
Unitax Association, 50 New Road, Great Baddow, Chelmsford, Essex CM2 7QT (Owen Ephraim).

Site-Value Land Taxation
Land Policy Council, 7 Kings Road, Teddington, Middlesex TW11 0QB (Fred Harrison).
Henry George Foundation, 177 Vauxhall Bridge Road, London SW1V 1EU.

Citizens' Income
Basic Income European Network (BIEN), Universite Catholique, Chaire Hoover, 3 Place Montesquieu, B-1348 Louvain-la-Neuve, Belgium (Philippe van Parijs).
Citizen's Income Research Group, St Philips Building, Sheffield Street, London WC2A 2EX (Rosalind Stevens-Strohmann).

Chapter 4: Money and Finance
Economic Reform Campaign, Gilnockie, 32 Kilbride Avenue, Dunoon, Argyll, Scotland PA23 7LH (Alan Armstrong).
IFF (Institute for Financial Services and Consumer Protection), Burchardstrasse 22, D-20095 Hamburg, Germany (Udo Reifner).
INAISE (International Association of Investors in the Social Economy), Rue d'Arlon 40, B-1000 Brussels, Belgium (Viviane Vandemeulebroucke).
LETSLINK, 2 Kent Street, Portsmouth PO1 3BS (Liz Shepherd).
Triodos Bank, Brunel House, 11 The Promenade, Bristol BS8 3NN (Glen Saunders).
UKSIF (UK Social Investment Forum), Vine Court, 112-116 Whitechapel Road, London E1 1JE (Penny Shepherd).

Chapter 5: The Global Economy
Catholic Institute for International Relations (CIIR), Unit 3, Canonbury Yard, 190a New North Road, London N1 7BJ.
IIED (International Institute for Environment and Development), 3 Endsleigh Street, London WC1H 0DD (Nick Robins).
UNED-UK, c/o United Nations Association's Sustainable Development Unit, 3 Whitehall Court, London SW1A 2EL (Derek Osborn).
World Development Movement, 25 Beehive Place, London SW9 7QR.

Appendix II

REFERENCES AND BIBLIOGRAPHY

This is an illustrative selection from a vast and growing literature.

Introduction
Schumacher, E.F. (1973) *Small Is Beautiful: a study of economics as if people mattered*, Blond & Briggs, London.
Schumacher, E.F. (1997) *A Guide for the Perplexed*, Jonathan Cape, London.
Schumacher, E.F (1979) *Good Work*, Jonathan Cape, London.
Schumacher, E.F. (1997) *This I Believe and Other Essays* (from the 1960s and '70s), Green Books, Dartington.

1. Transforming The System
Brandt, B. (1995) *Whole Life Economics: Revaluing Daily Life*, New Society Publishers, Philadelphia.
British Government Panel on Sustainable Development (1995, 1996 and 1997) *First, Second and Third Reports*, Department of the Environment, London.
Daly, H. and Cobb, J.(1990) *For the Common Good: Redirecting the Economy Towards Community, The Environment and a Sustainable Future*, Beacon Press, Boston.
Datta, A. (1997) *For a Quiet Revolution*, Papyrus, Calcutta.
Ekins, P. (ed.) (1986) *The Living Economy: A New Economics in the Making*, Routledge & Kegan Paul, London.
Harman, W. (1976) *An Incomplete Guide to the Future*, Stanford Alumni, California.
Henderson, H. (1996) *Building a Win-Win World: Life Beyond Global Economic Warfare*, Berrett-Koehler, San Francisco.
Higgins, R. (1978) *The Seventh Enemy: The Human Factor in the Global Crisis*, Hodder and Stoughton, London.
Jacobs, M. (1996) *The Politics of the Real World*, Earthscan, London.
Maslow, A.H. (1970), *Motivation and Personality*, Harper & Row, New York.
New Economics Foundation (quarterly) *New Economics*, NEF, London.

New Economics Foundation (1997) *Sustainable Economic Welfare in the UK,1950-1996* by Jackson,T., Marks,N., et al.
Roberts, Keith.V. (1985) *Design for a Market Economy*, privately published.
Robertson, J. (1978, 1983) *The Sane Alternative*, Robertson, Oxfordshire.
Robertson J. (1998) *Beyond The Dependency Culture*, Adamantine Press, London.
Sachs, W. et al (1998) *Greening The North: A Post-Industrial Blueprint for Ecology and Equity*, Zed Books, London.
von Weizsacker, E.U. (1994) *Earth Politics*, Zed Books, London.
von Weizsacker, E.U., Lovins, A. and Lovins, H. (1997) *Factor Four: Doubling Wealth, Halving Resource Use*, Earthscan, London.

2. A Common Pattern
Farming and Food
Paxton, A. (1994) *The Food Miles Report: The dangers of long distance food transport*, SAFE Alliance, London.
SAFE Alliance/CIIR Briefing (November 1996) *The Fischler Reforms: Options for the CAP*, SAFE/CIIR, London.
Shiva, V. (1991) *The Violence of the Green Revolution*, Zed Books, London.

Travel and Transport
Gleave, S.D. (1995) *Alternatives to Traffic Growth: The role of public transport and the future for freight*, Transport 2000, London.
Royal Commission on Environmental Pollution (1994) *Transport and the Environment*, HMSO, London.
Tourism In Focus, magazine of Tourism Concern, London.

Energy
See items at 1 above and 3 below.

Work, Livelihoods and Social Cohesion
'Civil Society: the Third Sector in Action' in *Development 1996:3*, Society for International Development, Rome.
Hulbert, A. (1996) *Towards an Economy of Care and Compassion*, Occasional Paper No.3, Ecumenical Association for Church and Society, Brussels.

Justice Office (1997) *Planning For Progress: Tackling Poverty, Unemployment and Exclusion,* Conference of Religious of Ireland, Dublin.
Rifkin, J. (1995) *The End of Work,* Putnam, New York.

Local Development
Colbourne, L. (ed.) (1996) *Sustainable Gloucestershire,* Vision 21, Cheltenham.
Douthwaite, R. (1996) *Short Circuit: Strengthening Local Economies for Security in an Unstable World,* Green Books, Devon.
Girardet, H. (1992 & 1996) *The Gaia Atlas of Cities: New Directions for Sustainable Urban Living,* Gaia Books, London.
Jopling J. and Girardet H. (1996) *Creating a Sustainable London,* Sustainable London Trust, London.
Morehouse, W. (ed., with Benello, C.G., Swann, R., Tunbull, S.) (1997) *Building Sustainable Communities,* Bootstrap Press, New York.
Pearce, J. (1993) *At the Heart of the Community Economy: Community enterprise in a changing world,* Gulbenkian Foundation, London.

Technology
Cooper, T. (1994) *Beyond Recycling: The Longer Life Option,* New Economics Foundation, London.

Business
Davis, J. (1991) *Greening Business: Managing for Sustainable Development,* Blackwell, Oxford.
Goyder, G. (1993) *The Just Enterprise,* Adamantine, London.
Hawken, P. (1993) *The Ecology of Commerce: How Business Can Save the Planet,* Harper Collins, New York.
Korten, D.C. (1995) *When Corporations Rule the World,* Berrett-Koehler, San Francisco.
Welford, R. and Starkey, R. (eds.) (1996) *Business and the Environment,* Earthscan, London.

3. Sharing Common Resources
A Restructured Tax System and a Citizen's Income
Kemball-Cook, D. et al (1991) *The Green Budget,* Greenprint, London.
Mulgan, G. and Murray, R. (1993) *Reconnecting Taxation,* Demos, London.

Ecotax Reform
DIW, German Institute for Economic Research (1994) *Ecological Tax Reform Even If Germany Has To Go It Alone*, Economic Bulletin, Vol.37, Gower, Aldershot.

Ekins, P. (1996) *Environmental Taxes and Charges: National Experiences and Plans*. European Foundation for the Improvement of Living and Working Conditions, Dublin.

European Environment Agency (1996) *Environmental Taxes: Implementation and Environmental Effectiveness*, Environmental Issues Series No.1, Copenhagen.

European Commission (1993) *Growth, Competitiveness, Employment: The Challenges and Ways Forward into the 21st Century*, Brussels.

Friends of the Earth (1996) *Green Dividends: Why the Chancellor should invest in Ecotax Reform*, Friends of the Earth, London.

Norwegian Green Tax Commission (1996) *Policies for a Better Environment and High Employment*, Norwegian Government, Oslo.

O'Riordan, T. (ed.) (1997) *Ecotaxation*, Earthscan, London.

von Weizsacker, E.U. and Jesinghaus, J. (1992) *Ecological Tax Reform*, Zed Books.

Site-Value Land Taxation
Gaffney, M. and Harrison F. (1994) *The Corruption of Economics*, Shepheard-Walwyn, London.

George, H. (1878) *Progress and Poverty*, Hogarth Press, London (1953 edition).

Harrison F. (ed.) (1998) *The Losses of Nations: Deadweight Politics versus Public Rent Dividends*, Othila Press, London.

Land and Liberty (quarterly magazine), Henry George Foundation, London.

David Richards, *The Land Value of Britain, 1985-1990*, Economic and Social Science Research Association, London.

Citizen's Income (or Basic Income)
Basic Income Newsletter (quarterly), Basic Income European Network.

Brittan, S. and Webb, S. (1990) *Beyond the Welfare State: An Examination of Basic Incomes in a Market Economy*, Aberdeen University Press.

Citizen's Income Bulletin (quarterly), Citizen's Income Research Group.

Clark, C. and Healy, J. (1997) *Pathways to a Basic Income*, CORI, Dublin.
Parker, H. (1991) *Basic Income and the Labour Market*, CI Research Group.
Parker, H. (1993) *Citizen's Income and Women*, ditto.
Schutz, R. (1996) *The $30,000 Solution: A guaranteed annual income for every American*, Fithian Press, California.
van Parijs, P. (1992) *Arguing for Basic Income: Ethical Foundations for a Radical Reform*, Verso Press, London.

Public Spending
Myers, N. (1998) *Perverse Subsidies: Their Nature, Scale and Impacts*, International Institute for Sustainable Development, Canada.
Wuppertal Bulletin, Summer 1997, *Guide to the Global Subsidies Jungle*.

4. Money and Finance
Armstrong, Alan. D (1996) *To Restrain the Red Horse: The Urgent Need for Radical Economic Reform*, Towerhouse Publishing, Dunoon, Scotland.
Greco, T.H. (1994) *New Money for Healthy Communities*, Greco, Tucson, Arizona.
Hayek, F.A. (1978) *Denationalisation of Money*, Institute of Economic Affairs, London.
Hoogendijk, W. (1991) *The Economic Revolution: towards a sustainable future by freeing the economy from money-making*, Greenprint, London.
Jacobs, J. (1984) *Cities and the Wealth of Nations: Principles of Economic Life*, Random House, New York.
Kennedy, M. (1995) *Interest and Inflation-Free Money: Creating an Exchange Medium that Works for Everybody and Protects the Earth*, New Society, Philadelphia.
Lietaer. B.A. (1996) *The Future of Money*, unpublished draft.
New Economics Foundation (1996) *Money Matters: Taking Charge of our Money, our Values and our Lives*, resource list and annotated bibliography, NEF, London.
Tomlinson, J. (1993) *Honest Money: A Challenge to Banking*, Helix Editions, Oxon.
Walker, P. et al (1996) *LETS on low income*, NEF, London.

5. The Global Economy

Brown, M.B. (1993) *Fair Trade*, Zed Books, London.

Cleveland, H., Henderson, H. and Kaul I. (eds.) (1995) *The United Nations at Fifty: Policy and Financing Alternatives*, Special Issue of Futures, Vol.27, No.2.

Commission on Global Governance (1995) *Our Global Neighbourhood*, Oxford University Press, Oxford.

Ekins, P. (1993) *Trading Off the Future*, New Economics Foundation, London.

Ekins, P. (1995) *Harnessing Trade to Sustainable Development*, Green College Centre for Environmental Policy and Understanding, Oxford.

Keynes, J.M. (1933) 'National Self-Sufficiency' in Moggridge D (ed.) *The Collected Writings of J.M. Keynes*, Macmillan, London.

Lang, T. and Hines, C. (1993) *The New Protectionism: Protecting the Future Against Free Trade*, Earthscan, London.

NEF/CIIR (1997) *Open Trading: options for effective monitoring of corporate codes of conduct*, New Economics Foundation and CIIR, London.

World Commission on Environment and Development (1987) *Our Common Future*, Oxford University Press.

THE SCHUMACHER SOCIETY

The Society was founded in 1977, following the death of economist and philosopher E. F. Schumacher. It promotes good economic practice, human-scale development and ecological and spiritual values, and contributes to new thinking and action on key issues of the new millennium. In our current social and cultural predicament we need not just ad hoc campaigning but also sound philosophical frameworks. Schumacher helped create such a framework and the Society sees its role in developing and applying it.

Some of the concepts formulated by Schumacher and his coworkers have found their way into national legislation and international agreements such as Agenda 21. However, most of these stop short of aiming for *real sustainability*, which is the Society's primary concern; in this context, we affirm the validity of the concepts of 'small is beautiful', 'connectedness' and 'quality of life', in contrast to 'standard of living', as a measure of human welfare.

To achieve its aims, the Society organises lectures in cities across the UK. The Bristol *Schumacher Lectures* have attracted large audiences every October since 1979 and have been dubbed by the Guardian 'the premier environmental gathering in the UK'. Annual lectures are also being held in Manchester and Liverpool, and soon in other cities in the UK. The publication of *Schumacher Briefings* is our latest initiative and we are aiming to produce three a year. They will provide concise information and rigorous clarity of explanation on key issues of our time. We hope that the Briefings will become essential reading for all concerned with creating a sustainable relationship between people and planet. They will offer:
- background information and an overview of the issue concerned
- an understanding of the state of play in the UK and elsewhere
- best practice examples of relevance to the issue under discussion
- an overview of policy implications and implementation.

The Briefings will be available from the Society individually and by subscription; the 12-page *Schumacher Newsletter*, published three times a year, gives information on the Society's work and that of affiliated organisations. For more information and membership details, contact:

The Schumacher Society, Foxhole Dartington, Devon TQ9 6EB
Phone/fax: 01803 865051

THE NEW ECONOMICS FOUNDATION

The New Economics Foundation (NEF) is an independent research institute based in London. It was set up in 1986 as the organising body for The Other Economic Summit (the People's Summit) now an annual conference which happens at the same time and place as the G8 Economic Summit. The People's Summit takes place in May 1998 with the involvement of over 50 organisations. NEF has become a centre for developing and promoting innovative work and practical approaches to economics which are responsive to social, ethical and environmental issues. Its work has two interconnected strands: promoting accountability-based performance in business and other civil organisations, and promoting community economic initiatives which emphasise self-help, sustainability and quality of life.

Its recent work includes:
• Helping to introduce Local Exchange Trading Systems to the UK.
• Working with local communities to develop indicators to measure quality of life which challenge conventional economic wisdom about social performance.
• Pioneering with others the recent developments in social auditing, to allow organisations to measure, report on and improve their own social performance.
• Publishing *Community Works!* - a do-it-yourself guide to local community economic action.

By joining NEF as a supporter you will get:
• a quarterly magazine, *New Economics* • the latest information on alternatives from fair trade to ethical investment • practical guidance on what you can do • imagination and hope!

Annual rates are: Low/unwaged/student supporter, £8; Regular supporter, £18; Core supporter, £130; Publications package, £75.

For further information and to join please contact:

New Economics Foundation,
First Floor, Vine Court, 112-116 Whitechapel Road, London E1 1JE.
Tel: 0171 377 5696 Fax: 0171 377 5720
E-mail: neweconomics@gn.apc.org   UK Registered Charity No 1055254
Web site: http://sosig.ac.uk/neweconomics/newecon.html

THE SCHUMACHER BOOK SERVICE
The Best Books On Ecological Thought And Practice, Mailed Anywhere

We believe the world needs new ideas, and that good books are a powerful way to spread them. But for the general reader it can be hard to find books in our field which truly reward the time and concentration they demand. With over 300 new English language titles appearing each year on environmental issues, ecology or sustainable development, it's easy to get overwhelmed.

At the Schumacher Book Service we offer a route through the maze. Based on our own reading of new and classic titles, we sell a selected list of great books from both mainstream and alternative publishers. Spanning topics as diverse as biology, economics, agriculture, politics, psychology, philosophy, and the arts of daily life, our selections offer a sampling from the finest books available.

We now have customers all over the world; committed readers who value our recommendations, reasonable prices and prompt mail order service. If you would like to join them, please contact us for a free copy of our latest catalogue and special offers:

The Schumacher Book Service, Foxhole SB1, Dartington, Totnes, Devon TQ9 6EB, UK schumacher@gn.apc.org
Phone/fax 0800 458 8155 (UK only) or +44 1803 868-547

GREEN BOOKS LTD

We publish and distribute many titles that relate to the subjects discussed in this Briefing; in particular Richard Douthwaite's two books *The Growth Illusion*, on the perils of unrestrained economic growth, and *Short Circuit*, a comprehensive guide to local economic development; also *This I Believe and other essays*, a selection of E.F. Schumacher's essays published in Resurgence magazine. For our latest catalogue, please contact us:

Green Books, Foxhole, Dartington, Totnes, Devon TQ9 6EB
Phone/fax: 01803 863843 greenbooks@gn.apc.org
www.greenbooks.co.uk